How to Start & Maintain a Profitable Sewing Business:
Making Money with Your Sewing Skills

Copyright 2006 by Becky Reed

Published by BookSurge, LLC, an Amazon.com company
5341 Dorchester Road, Suite 16
North Charleston, South Carolina 29418

Manufactured in the United States of America

ISBN 1-4196-2454-7
LCCN 2006901139

How to Start & Maintain a Profitable Sewing Business

Making Money with Your Sewing Skills

by Becky Reed

How to Start & Maintain a Profitable Sewing Business: Making Money with Your Sewing Skills

Table of Contents

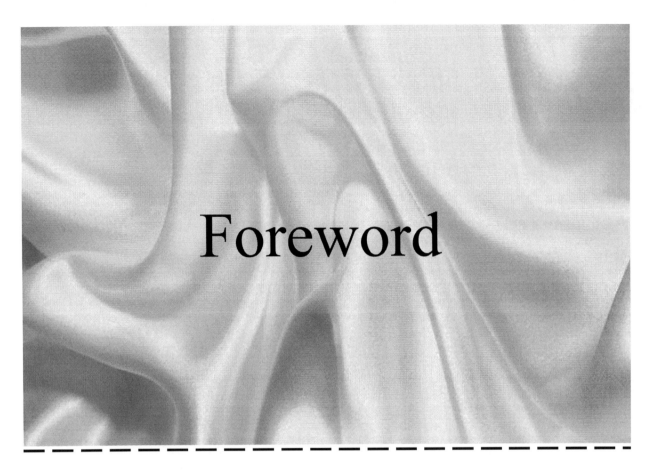

Foreword

There are endless things that a person can sew and sell. There is always the need for clothing, bags, toys, costumes, alterations, and so much more. If you have the skills to sew well, there is a market for your skills.

How you go about marketing those skills and creating a successful business is what this book is all about. This book will show you how to make your ideas more concrete, how to organize them, and how to execute them. You may already have some business experience—this book will deliver a viewpoint about the finer points of business to which you may not have given much thought. You may have no business experience at all—this book will give you a good start towards putting together your ideas, business plan, and more.

There are so many details to which an entrepreneur must pay attention in order to build a successful business, and to reduce the risk that is expected as a new business is started. If you are creative, and do not normally think about "the business end of things," then dealing with paperwork, customer complaints, shipping problems, and the like, may scare you away from taking your creative skills to the next level—to make money.

As long as you have passion for what you do, stay organized, pay attention to detail, and be persistent about your goals, success can be achieved over time, and you can build and maintain a successful sewing business.

**Section 1
Evaluating
Your Skills**

SKILLS

What Do You Know & What Are You Good At?

For many people, sewing skills are self taught. Most people who sew are women, but there is a growing trend that shows men are taking hold of the needle and thread and being creative.

Of the small percentage of people that have a formal education in some area of sewing, there are only a handful that pursue sewing as a career. Some go on to be theatrical costumers, clothing designers, or go to work for a large company sewing products.

How Well Can You Sew?

There is a distinct difference between hand-crafted and homemade. You will need to rate your sewing skills honestly, or have someone that you trust give you feedback on projects you have created. Your goal should be to achieve the "hand-crafted" look in whatever you sew.

Stitches should be uniform and straight; you should know your equipment well enough to be able to adjust it as necessary. You should have all of the necessary tools to complete a project, as well as the uninterrupted time. Do not cut corners, or use low-grade materials, as these things stand out and look unprofessional.

Unfinished seams, threads hanging loose, seams pulling apart, and crooked seam lines stand out and are poor quality. If you do not have the patience to pay attention to details

such as these on a regular basis, stop reading here, and reconsider your reasons for wanting to go into business for yourself.

Quality should never be sacrificed for lack of time or lack of attention to detail. Customers will notice these things, and it will impact your business. Not everyone has "couture" sewing skills, but if you take your time, and have the necessary equipment to get the job done correctly, then you can create a high quality item, and be proud to sell it under your name brand.

If your goal is to sell clothing, try creating a wardrobe for yourself or someone you know. Get opinions from family and friends on different aspects of your creations. Make a checklist of things to look for so that they know what to critique (see Section 9, Quality Control, for a checklist).

Do not take criticism too personally. Remember, you are trying to improve your skills and if you want to improve, then you have to acknowledge where there are potential problems.

As you work, note the amount of time it takes you to complete an item, as well as how much in materials you use (including mistakes). Being honest with yourself will give you the true picture of your readiness for going into business.

READINESS

If you love to sew projects around the house or the occasional garment or doll, and you also sew for enjoyment, you are likely a sewing hobbyist. You may have quite a stash of thread, materials, and notions in a spare, peaceful room that you have dedicated to your craft.

In your mind, replace your regular daily activities with sewing. Replace the fabric stash with inventory. Trade out craft magazines for vendor catalogs, customer receipts, and sewing journals. Replace the peaceful workspace with a ringing phone and a complaining customer. Orders are stacked up waiting for your attention. And still, your personal life, and regular daily stresses go on...

Could you handle this day in and day out without getting burned out? Would you wind up hating your beloved hobby? Have you created a monster? All good questions to ask yourself before starting a sewing business.

Once you start investing money and resources into creating a sewing business, to see any kind of return on your investment, you will need to put in the time and effort that it takes to make it successful. This could mean many hours, working on customer orders, forgoing family get-togethers, or rearranging your personal schedule to accommodate your new business schedule.

On the other hand, once it is established, your business may allow you more time to spend with family, or to pursue personal endeavors.

Shown: Hand Knitting & Professional Knitting Machine

You may enjoy the freedom you have gained by not working for someone else. You can set your own hours, and you have complete control over your own success. But you will need discipline and a consistent routine to make it all work.

Many people who go into business for themselves keep their regular job for financial security, to help fund investments in the new business, and to pay their regular personal bills while the new business grows. This is a wise decision if you can handle the hours.

Making the choice to go into business should be looked at realistically. Be honest with yourself, and decide whether your yearning to create is just a hobby, or if you truly have the discipline that is necessary to build a successful business and manufacture on a large scale.

Once you have made the decision to go into business for yourself, allow at least one year to devote to establishing your business, possibly longer, depending on what you are selling. Gain the support of family and friends and focus on your success!

**Section 2
Ideas To Put
You To Work**

IDEAS

So What Do You Want To Sew For a Living?

If you do not have in mind what you want to sew for your new business, think about what you like to sew—not just what is popular. What types of things are you good at making? What pleases you the most? Clothing? Dolls? Animal toys? Here are some ideas that you might consider sewing, or may give you alternative ideas:

Clothing
- Sports & Casual Wear
- Historic Costumes
- Halloween Costumes
- Business Wear (men's or women's)
- Lingerie (practical & novelty)
- Sleepwear
- Swimwear
- Formalwear (bridal, prom, special occasion)
- Kitchen Aprons
- Hats
- Children's Clothing & Diapers

Handbags (purses, totes, backpacks)

Children's Toys & Accessories

Animal Toys

Holiday Ornaments & Decorations

General Crafts (scrapbook covers & pages, decorations, useful or not-so-useful objects)

Household Items
- Kitchen Linens (tablecloths, placemats, napkins, appliance covers, oven mitts)
- Bedroom Linens (sheets, pillowcases, decorative coverings, pillows)
- Bath Accessories
- Living Room (chair slipcovers, pillows, decorative coverings)
- Drapery
- Quilts
- Nursery Accessories
- General Upholstery

Tents & Pavilions

Outdoor Furniture Coverings

Car Seat Cushions & Vehicle Coverings

Custom Embroidery

Alterations & Other Custom Work

Teaching & Demonstrations

Write down other ideas that may come to you as you read this list. There are so many things that you can sew, your options are limited only by your abilities, and you can always learn how to sew more.

To get more ideas, visit craft fairs, read sewing magazines, scour the internet for possible markets, and think about ways to improve what you see other people or companies making. Try sewing a few different things, and decide what you would like to sew for your business, keeping track of time, ease of sewing, and materials involved in each project. Sew what you love.

**Section 3
Deciding On Your
Product Line**

DECISIONS

Hypothetically, let us say you have decided to sew children's clothing for your business. You may have your own children, or know other people with children, and you love making clothing for them.

Now, you need to decide what type of children's clothing you will create. Sleepwear… playwear… special occasion… the list can go on and on. Maybe you want to create an entire line of children's clothing? Maybe you will want to specialize in sleepwear for infants only. Sometimes, it can be difficult to know what to focus on; what the right choice will be for you. It is an important decision, because you will be devoting time, money, and other resources to this new endeavor.

Do you have time to make your own original designs for the clothing? Do you know anything about pattern drafting? You will need to design your own patterns for the clothing (see Section 11, Copyrights & Intellectual Property).

Will you need help making the clothing on a large scale? Do you want to keep this a small enterprise, or do you want to manufacture your designs to sell nationally?

Once you decide on the item you will be sewing, make up several different prototypes of the design, different colors, styles, etc. Take some digital photos of the items, and examine how they look. Have your friends and family take a look at the items and ask them to give relevant feedback. What could you change?

What could you improve? How is what you have made better than what is already for sale on the market?

Let us go back to the hypothetical line of children's clothing. You may be discouraged that there are already companies out there that sell children's clothing on a large scale. You may not think that you can compete with a large corporation, such as Anne Geddes™ , or Zutano™ - or even Target™ . Here is an analogy: Think of the market as a pail, where the big companies fill it with large rocks. There is room around the rocks for you to fill in. Your products could compliment the existing products on the market, and fill needs not being met by large companies—a niche market if you will.

Figure out who your customers will be. What are their needs? Where can you "fill in" where large companies do not?

The small business **can** compete with larger corporations. There are many people who would rather support you and your business, than give their money to a large corporation who may use sweatshop labor or even pollute the environment. You **do** have a chance! So what if it has been done before—do it **better**!

Section 4
Business Essentials

PLANNING

There are many businesses that do not have a business plan. The business owner may not see the need for a business plan as it may be a family-run business, passed down generations, where the owner lives and breathes the everyday happenings, and shoulders the burden of financial downfalls. Or it may be a small business whose owner is someone who just is not into all the paperwork that a business plan represents. So why bother?

Business owners should create a plan that explains their business strategy and goals. When you draw up a business plan, you are forced to put your ideas on paper, rank your priorities, and clarify your objectives. It makes you plan for the future rather than just worry about coping with it one day.

Having a solid business plan for your business will keep you organized and also give you a clear, honest picture of how your business will operate—and whether or not it will succeed. This is why many financial lending institutions require that you have a business plan in order to process an application for a business loan. Your business plan should be kept up to date as your business grows, just like your personal résumé.

The business plan is one of the most paperwork-intensive parts of a business. If you are looking for financing, you will almost always have to have a business plan and personal résumé ready to be reviewed by lenders.

There are many useful software programs that will make writing a business plan easier, and there are also people available that will put your plan together for a fee. Business Plan Pro™ by Palo Alto Software is an excellent program to assist you in building your own business plan.

The following list may be tailored to suit any retail, mail order, or internet enterprise. It will give you an honest picture of your business. The list has many key points to examine and answer. This may seem daunting, but it is well worth the effort to get everything down on paper for this step of the planning process.

Note that the questions listed are not the business plan, but a tool to help you build one. Plan on taking several hours to put together your final business plan. You may be able to answer these questions relatively quickly, or this exploration may prompt you to ask more questions as you read through the text.

Business Plan Development: Some Questions...

1. Description of store or workshop location — what is it like in the area? Home studio? (foot traffic, visibility)
2. Competition analysis - who are your competitors and what do they sell?
3. How would you describe your customers?
4. Are there any leasing or rental agreement details for your studio or storefront?
5. What does your storefront or website look like?
6. What is the layout of your store or workshop?
7. What type of equipment will you keep on hand?
8. What is the value of your equipment?
9. What type of inventory will you stock?
10. Will you accept custom orders?
11. What does your line of merchandise include? (List pricing with each item)
12. Where do you purchase your merchandise or supplies?
13. Do you have a large assortment of vendors?
14. What if one of the vendors you used went out of business? Do you have a backup?
15. What is your opening inventory count and dollar value of all your stock? (notions, thread, fabric, etc.)
16. How will you keep track of your inventory and supplies in stock?
17. Do you offer any special discounts?
18. Do you offer customers credit?
19. What does your one-year promotional calendar look like?
20. What is your advertising budget?
21. What is your selection of media for advertising?
22. Do you have a seasonal promotional program or holiday marketing strategy in place?
23. Do you have any cooperative advertising efforts with others in the industry?
24. Have you been through any customer service programs or educational seminars?
25. What is your level of experience in this business?
26. Do you have employees?
27. If so, have the employees been trained in customer service?
28. What level of sewing expertise do your employees have?
29. What are the job specifications for your employees?
30. What are your sources of prospective employees?
31. What are some benefits and incentives to offer employees?
32. What will motivate your employees to do their best?
33. What type of bookkeeping method will you use? (cash or accrual)
34. Do you have a balance sheet? (list of assets, liabilities, regular expenses, etc.)
35. What are your expenses? (power, phone, postage, taxes, insurance, etc.)
36. What are your cash flow projections? (be realistic!)
37. If you have an existing website, have you examined the statistics on its traffic with your host?
38. What websites do your potential customers use to find you?
39. Are you well indexed with search engines? (what is your website's page ranking on various search terms)
40. Do you have a tax consultant or bookkeeper?
41. Are you pricing your sale items high enough to provide yourself with a living wage?
42. What is your return/refund policy?
43. What methods of research will you do to examine your competition, market analysis, and pricing structure?
44. Will you accept credit cards?
45. What is your back up plan if your hosting service for your website is down?
46. How will you fulfill orders when you are ill or have family responsibilities?
47. What are your plans for new products?
48. Do you have business insurance? (some homeowners policies are not enough)

Marketing Your Business: Marketing is not just advertising

Marketing is a combination of several factors called a *market mix*. If you have taken a formal marketing course or have read marketing books, you will know that a market mix includes the product, price, promotion, and distribution. The market mixed is used to describe how a business owner will combine these areas into an overall marketing program.

> Successful marketing is the process of attracting customers, and retaining a solid base of satisfied return customers.

Marketing is not just publishing a miniscule classified ad and hoping someone will buy from you if they see your ad buried in the back of the local newspaper. Deciding on your product, pricing it to sell, putting it in a place where people will notice it, and how you promote your products will all determine your success.

All business activities should be directed toward satisfying customer needs. Profitable sales volume is more important than maximum sales volume.

To best use these principles, a small business should:

- Determine the needs of their customers through market research
- Analyze their competitive advantages to develop a market strategy
- Select specific markets to serve by target marketing
- Determine how to satisfy customer needs by identifying a market mix

A successful marketing strategy identifies customer needs in which a business can better serve than its competitors, and tailors product offerings, prices, distribution, promotional efforts, and services toward those market needs. A good strategy helps a business focus on the target markets it can serve best.

Small business owners usually have limited resources to spend on marketing their businesses. Concentrating efforts on one or a few key market segments gets the most return from investments.

Some Methods of Promotion:
- Internet, website, search engine indexing
- Word of mouth
- Business cards, brochures, flyers
- Trade shows & craft fairs, sponsorship
- Promotional gifts
- Television, radio, print, other media
- Signature lines within e-mail, listing a link or other business contact information

Research & Development
Who is your competition? Have you looked around on the internet, in your local phonebook, at your local mall, to see who is doing something similar to what you want to do?

What makes your competitors successful? Where could you improve upon their ideas? Are there methods and materials on the market that would make it less expensive for you to construct your product, thereby making you more profitable?

Pricing of Your Product Line
Stay competitive in the market with your product pricing. Check competitor websites and visit competitor stores. Unless you want business to slow down (and sometimes you

may want things to slow down if you are too busy), keep prices reasonable, but with a good markup.

Remember to pay yourself a living wage. Aim for at least 50-500% profit, or more depending on the market you are targeting. Charge what you are worth. You have to allow money for yourself, taxes and expenses.

Considering the costs of finer fabrics, price your creations accordingly. Make sure that if you miss a sale at the local fabric store that your prices will allow you enough of a markup to buy fabric at full price if you had to, and still clear a profit.

An example of this scenario:

Velvet gown	$450
Velvet regular price	$18/yard
Velvet sale price	$11/yard
Yardage needed:	7 yards
Notions:	$10
Labor:	$120
Profit w/ sale fabric:	$243
Profit w/fabric not on sale:	$194

Figure pricing to include extra notions and fabric if necessary. Keep in mind that sometimes spools of thread can cost $6 or $7 each depending on the thread quality. Trims can run from $1 per yard to well over $15 per yard.

If you are overwhelmed by too much work, mark up the pricing of your merchandise. This slows "the economy" down to a reasonable flow. When you need more work, drop prices back to normal, or lower prices to increase business.

During slow times, sell through online auction sites, making sure there is a reasonable reserve price set on each auction (see Section 6, Auctions) so that your listing fees are covered.

Your Business Name
Naming your business is almost like naming a child. Some people spend months trying to figure out a name for their business, while others new its name all along.

If you are having trouble coming up with a business name, start by clustering words pertaining to your business. You might also try looking through a thesaurus or dictionary to find words similar to those you have already thought about. If you will be building a website, consider the domain names that are available when naming your business.

Talk to relatives or friends to get ideas. Try looking through books, periodicals and even foreign resources that might have catchy phrases. If you decide to use words from a foreign language, make sure they can be easily understood and pronounced.

Register your business name with state and local agencies, and check to see if your city requires a business license or other declaration for tax purposes.

Your business logo
You do not have to choose a logo for your business, though it can help people remember your business. Think about the chevrons in the Chevron™ gas logo, or the Pepsi™ ball. These are all marketing strategies that work well. They are catchy and colorful, and people remember them – almost like a bad jingle. Read through advertising books to get ideas.

The logo for your business should sum up what your business is all about. If you design your own logo, make sure that it is not too busy or difficult to figure out. The more you try to cram into a small space, the harder it will be to read. Shapes and symbols are eye-catching, and so are bright colors. Experiment with different ideas until you find the right logo.

Cost Analysis of Your Product Line

Make a worksheet and list all of the materials and notions required for each piece of merchandise you carry in your product line. List the price you will charge your customers for each item, as well as the time involved to make each item. Sometimes, you may need to do this as you complete a project, and projects may vary. From this list, figure out how much each item will cost to make and price each item to make the best profit and still be competitive (see chart on the next page).

When you start your sewing business, save your profits and reinvest them back into your business by purchasing materials and equipment you may find on sale. For example, if you know you buy a lot of muslin and it is normally $1.99 per yard, and you find a sale for 99¢ per yard, you should stock up and take advantage of the sale.

Buying materials in bulk will help save money in the long run, but watch out for minimum order requirements from vendors. For example, you may only need one case of fiberfill, but the required minimum order may be 20 cases. You may be able use 20 cases over time, but do you have the money to buy this many cases, and do you have the room to store them once you have them? Will you have to sacrifice buying something else to make a bulk purchase?

> *The basic premise of capitalism:*
> *Make & sell your products. Reinvest your profits to make more products, and larger profits, and your business will grow.*

Popular Marketing Books

Find these popular books about Marketing at your local library, or buy them online.

Guerrilla Marketing: Secrets for Making Big Profits from Your Small Business (Guerrilla Marketing)—by Jay Conrad Levinson; ISBN 0395906253

The 22 Immutable Laws of Marketing—by Al Ries, Jack Trout; ISBN 0887306667

Marketing Management (textbook)—by Philip Kotler; ISBN 0130336297

Marketing for Dummies—by Alexander Hiam; ISBN 0764556002

Success Secrets of the Online Marketing Superstars—by Mitch Meyerson; ISBN 1419505017

Here is a simple worksheet that you can use to figure out what the real costs are to make a product. A blank sheet is included in Appendix B. It will also give a you a clear idea of what your profit will be. When figuring the cost analysis for a product, list the materials, the quantity needed, the supplier, cost per item, and shipping and handling charges, if applicable. Also, list any other things you may need to remember about the vendor, such as minimum order requirements, phone numbers, etc. If you must buy in bulk, then divide the bulk quantity by the price you paid to figure out the unit price. For example, if you must buy 25 yards of muslin at $25, then you are paying $1 per yard. Remember to include shipping in the total if applicable. If you only use 3 yards for a product with no shipping, then the cost is $3 for that material. Also, remember to factor in the cost of the trip to pick something up; gas, travel expenses, etc.

Make one of these worksheets for each product and prototype you plan to sew and sell. Change it as your product line changes, and keep them for future reference. These worksheets will be helpful when you develop your business plan, or need to look at your "bottom line" to see how well your business is doing, what you are really paying for materials, and whether or not you need to readjust your pricing structure.

Simple Cost Analysis Worksheet for a Garment

Project Name:	Wedding Gown				
Materials	**Quantity Needed**	**Unit Price + Shipping**	**Total Price**	**Vendor**	**Notes**
Silk Fabric	7 yards	$9/yd + $7 Shipping	$70	SyFabrics	Color: white
Thread	2 spools	$4 each	$8	Jo-Ann	JP Coats
Lining & Interlining	2 yards cotton duck 2 yards cotton	$2.50/yard each	$10	WalMart	
Boning	2 yards	$2.50/yard	$5	Farthingales	Free shipping
Grommets for back lacings	24 sets	.06 per set (144 @ $8.00) includes shipping	$1.44	American Trim	size 0 for lacings www.atrim.com
Metallic Trim	10 yards	$1.50/yard + $5 shipping	$20	Calontir Trim	Item #142111
Labor	6 hours	$20/hour	$120		Pay self
Total cost			$234.44		
Customer Price			$475		
Profit			$240.56		Reinvest

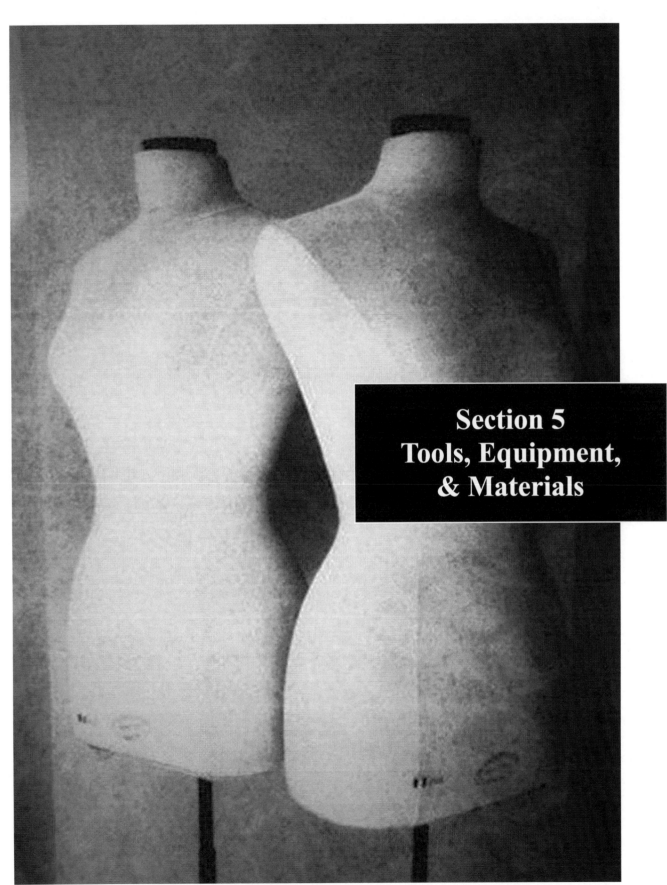

**Section 5
Tools, Equipment,
& Materials**

TOOLS

Each sewing business is different. Every person has their workspace set up differently, and you should do what works best for you, using the space available. Listed here are some ideas for tools, equipment, and supplies. The usefulness of each item will depend upon what you are sewing.

Having the right tools and equipment to complete a job makes work more efficient and enjoyable. If you save time, that means you are saving money.

Sewing Machines & Sergers
To reduce downtime, buy more than one sewing machine. Buy a back up for those times when your main sewing machine may need service so that you are not without a way to produce your products as needed.

You can look for back up machines at thrift stores, garage sales and online auctions, but there is one caveat: make sure it works. Even better, buy from a reputable sewing machine dealer and try sewing with the machine before you buy it. Have the salesperson demonstrate how the machine works, and make sure you understand all functions. Also ask about warranties.

Make sure that you maintain your machines and keep them clean. Never blow out thread fuzz; it only packs it up in the machine tighter. Buy a small coarse bristle brush to sweep out the areas where fuzz collects. Crafter's pipe cleaners also work well for cleaning. Also, buy good quality lightweight machine oil and use it sparingly. Maintain your machines often. Ask your sewing machine dealer or repair technician to show you the proper way to oil and maintain your machines.

Work Table & Chair
It is extremely important to have a comfortable, ergonomic work area. Consider buying or building a worktable that is comfortable for your height. If you will be cutting out many yards of fabric, pinning designs, or stooping over the table a lot, you will prevent back strain if your table is the correct height.

A cutting table should be heavy, smooth, and free of clutter. It should be wide and long enough for pattern drafting, as well as for unrolling bolts of fabric and for pinning and cutting designs.

Mount a yardstick on your cutting table for measuring fabrics, add a thick glass cutting board to protect the surface. If you do not have a convenient electrical outlet, add a power strip on the end where you can plug in an iron, glue gun, or small clip-on fan. A self-healing cutting mat for use with a rotary cutting blade is also useful addition to your work table.

Buy an adjustable drafting chair with a soft back and well padded seat. A metal ring base will last many more years than a plastic base. Make sure the chair is sturdy and comfortable. Buy one with wheels for added mobility, and add an anti-static mat underneath.

Hand Tools

Adjust this list to suit your project needs:

- sharp scissors in different sizes
- various sizes of hand-sewing needles
- various sized sewing machine needles
- tracer wheel
- rotary cutting wheel
- craft knife & blades
- glue gun
- chalk pencils & fabric markers
- pattern transfer paper
- fusible web
- sharp pinking shears
- pins and cushions
- small gauge ruler, regular ruler
- safety pins
- soft and metal tape measures
- extra bobbins
- artist's bone or letter opener (for pushing out sewn corners and edges)
- spool adapter—this allows you to use large serger thread spools on a standard sewing machine
- pliers, small screw drivers, and other clean, small hand tools

Lighting

Good lighting is essential for detail work to prevent eye strain. A 300-watt halogen torch or "torchiere" lamp that is adjustable using a dimmer switch, as well as a lamp that uses 75-watt bulbs are excellent sources for lighting your work area. Fluorescent lights are efficient on costs and light output.

Also, an adjustable desk light affixed to a shelf above your sewing machine will help you see details while you work.

Art Supplies

Art supplies are handy if you have to sketch designs, stamp fabric or paint various projects. Have on hand calligraphy pens, marker pens, metallic pens, colored pencils, #2 pencils, crayons and ballpoint pens, and measuring devices.

Organizers

Plastic craft organizers are wonderful for storing small notions and beads, and will keep everything neat and separated. Buy a wooden thread tree to keep your thread spools organized and ready when you need them. A bobbin organizer will keep full bobbins from becoming messy. A portable sewing tray or tackle box is handy if you want to work outside your workshop, at a customer's house, or wherever you may be.

Dispensers

For ease of dispensing, use wall-mounted or shelf-mounted dispensers with wooden dowels for ribbon, trims, bulk seam binding rolls and other spooled materials.

Ironing Station

Consider buying a good quality ironing board that can be attached to a wall or door to store it out of the way. Make sure the board is well padded, and clean. Keep your iron clean, and check its surface every time you need to use it. Ironing fabric that is not color fast can leave a thin layer of dye on the iron face that will ruin fabrics during the next use.

Other useful pressing equipment might include a misting spray bottle (for controlled steaming), tailor's pressing ham, velvet pressing board, and a sleeve or cuff pressing board.

Hangers

Buy good sturdy wooden hangers with metal clips for hanging heavy garments or fabrics. Clothespins are handy when you need an extra hand, or need to keep items from slipping off a hanger. When using clothespins, slip a fold or two of tissue paper underneath the clip end to prevent damage to the fabric.

Clean-up

Have on hand a vacuum cleaner, magnets to pick up stray pins, and a static-charged duster to pick up lint and dust.

Dress Forms for Clothing Makers

It is handy to have adjustable dress forms of each size, (small, medium and large). There are several different types of dress forms available, and you should do thorough research, and read product reviews on each form before making a decision on what will work best for your needs.

Forms can be purchased new, used, or handmade. When purchasing a second-hand dress form, make sure it is complete and that no parts are missing.

If you like to iron garments and mold them while on the dress form (this is necessary for inserting some sleeves), then find a form that is resistant to water and heat. Pinnable forms are also helpful.

Uniquely You™ makes a dress form that is made from foam rubber that can be compressed to fit inside a zip-on cover that is adjusted to your needed measurements. It can be readjusted with some effort.

Wire form models from the 1960s are extremely useful and resizable for different body types. They are called "My Double" by Dritz™. These forms are made of a flexible mesh, and snap together in the center front and center back. Your customer can try them on and you can mold the form exactly to your customer's body during personalized fittings or you can adjust them to fit measurements a customer sends you for a project. These types of dress forms are no longer available new, but can be purchased through online auctions usually for less than $100 each. Add padding and an old t-shirt or covering for pinning designs directly on the form.

Dress forms that are adjusted by using dials may not be suitable for making certain garments, and are sometimes difficult to adjust body proportions without substantial pad-

ding. Bust line positions may vary, and this is difficult to correct. Research methods for making homemade dress forms, using materials such as Papier Mâchè, plaster, duct tape, and other supplies. There are also a number of businesses on the internet that provide custom-made forms.

File Cabinet

Store patterns, receipts, invoices and more in a cabinet sized suitably for your studio. Clear file boxes, and cardboard office file boxes also work well, though they are not as sturdy as a metal file.

Shelves

You may find that wall-mounted shelves will keep you organized and your work area clear. A tall bookcase may also be useful for storing supplies, as well as many sewing reference books and periodicals.

Computer

Upgrade your computer about once every two to five years. It is important to have a good working system because you may need to access the internet frequently, use software to create patterns, access picture files and word processing, or online banking.

Software

Quickbooks Pro™, Dreamweaver™, Netscape™ or Internet Explorer™ , Microsoft Office Suite™, My Label Designer™, Corel Draw™, Adobe Creative Suite™, and Photo Studio™, are all excellent software programs. They will save you time in creating documents, designing advertising and graphics, photo editing, bookkeeping, and more.

Keep current vendor catalogs and sewing magazines handy to read about the latest tools and supplies available for your sewing projects.

Fabrics

The fabric market (or sometimes referred to as the textiles market) is sometimes an unpredictable market. You never know when you will come across a good deal. Sometimes, you might find 100% linen material for $4 per yard on the web, but you might also be able to buy the same linen for $5 yard locally at a fabric store. Consider your shipping costs and quality when you mail order fabric or supplies.

Make sure to buy enough fabric to complete a project. If you buy too little, you may not be able to find more in the same dye lot again. If you buy too much, then you will have to store it, and it may not be enough to complete another project.

Look for quality fabrics without holes, stains, slubs, runs, and dirt. If you are buying an expensive, high-end fabric, ask the sales clerk to allow you to inspect the entire length for problems. This may be time consuming for long lengths of fabric, but it is well worth the time if you are spending a lot of money for the purchase.

Besides traditional textile vendors, check your local thrift stores and estate sales for drapes and other fabrics that you might be able to recycle for your projects.

Fabric Content

There are two different classes of fabrics: man-made (synthetic) and natural. Clothing made of natural fibers has better breathability than those made with synthetics, and are generally more comfortable to wear in various degrees of weather. Knowing a fabric's content will also help you determine the best methods of cleaning and pre-shrinking. If the content is unknown, conduct a burn text.

To conduct a burn test, snip a piece of fabric approximately 1" square. Using a lighter or candle, hold the fabric with a pair of tweezers and light it over a non-flammable surface in a well-ventilated area. Examine the quality and color of the flame, the odor produced, and the quality of the resulting ash.

Warnings: Use a small piece of fabric only. Hold the fabric with metal tweezers, not your fingers. Synthetic fabrics will ignite and melt and can cause serious burns, so be careful to keep them away from your skin while conducting tests. Always work in a safe, well-ventilated area with water and a fire extinguisher handy, and never leave a fire unattended!

Wool is a natural protein fiber. It does not burn easily. While burning, it smells similar to burning hair (because it is hair!). The ash produced is usually black.

Silk is a natural protein fiber that burns slowly. Silks smells like burning hair and produces little or no ash.

Cotton is a natural plant fiber. It burns readily with a yellow flame. It smells like burning paper or leaves. The ash produced is usually gray.

Linen is a natural plant (grass) fiber similar to cotton. Linen fibers burn slower than cotton fibers. Linen smells like burning leaves and usually produces a gray ash.

Rayon is a natural plant/wood fiber (cellulose), but is still a man-made fiber. Rayon produces very little, if any ash, and smells similar to burning paper.

Nylon is a synthetic fiber and melts as it burns. Nylon burns with a bluish flame and leaves hard beads rather than ash.

Polyester is a synthetic fiber and burns easily. Polyester leaves hard beads rather than ash. Many fabrics are made with polyester, and are usually blended. Blends will produce some ash. Smoke is usually black.

Storing Fabric

Fabrics should be stored in a dry, smoke-free and animal-free environment. Some people are allergic to dust from cigarettes and pet dander (not to mention the smell can be awful), so it is best never to expose your inventory to these contaminants. If fabric is stored in a moist location, such as a basement, it can mildew. To prevent fading, always protect fabrics from sun or constant bright light.

Wind your fabric on cardboard bolts, upholstery fabric roll cores, or wrapping paper roll cores. Velvets and fabrics with a pile should always be hung to protect fullness. Hangers for such fabrics will have sharp hooks to hang the fabric by the selvage.

Once your fabrics are on their hanger, bolt, or roll, cover them with a plastic bag or canvas covering to protect the fabric from dust and insects. Use clear, PVC-free plastic for easy identification. You can also store fabric bolts stacked on shelves, but make sure there is enough air space to circulate fresh air around the bolts to prevent mildew from general humidity, and always protect fabric from dust and light.

Keep track of the number of yards left of each type of fabric, just as a fabric store would inventory their supply. This will help you properly gauge the value and supply of your inventory, and help determine when you need to reorder.

Trims, laces and other narrow notions and fabrics should be stored on rolls or wound on cards. Save your old paper towel rolls and ribbons spools—they are perfect for keeping things neat and orderly.

Pre-Washing Fabrics

Depending upon what you will be making with your fabrics, you may want to pre-wash them before you start sewing. If you are making garments with the fabric, this will save your customer unnecessary stress over something that may have fit—that is until they wash it. Simply ironing 100% cotton fabric can make it shrink, so it is best to run these fabrics through a hot water wash cycle and then a high-heat dryer cycle to make sure they are stable. Washing will remove any unwanted chemicals from the fabric milling process. To prevent unraveling, hem the ends or tie them together before washing.

Section 6
Buying & Selling Using
Online Auctions

The most popular online auction websites on the internet:
eBay.com
Amazon.com
Overstock.com
Yahoo.com

Learn how to use auction sites to your advantage when
buying or selling products online.

AUCTIONS

Online auctions are an excellent resource for buying and selling products on the internet. There are many popular auction sites, each with their own set of rules and fee structures.

Selling Your Products

Online auctions are a wonderful way to start your business. Bidders are looking for a bargain, so you may not get full price for something you are trying to sell, but the exposure is worth the effort. Some people call auctions, "virtual garage sales." Auctions provide people with a unique way to locate one-of-a-kind items, as well as discounted merchandise.

Auctions usually run anywhere from one day up to 10 days. You will need to include a good quality photo of the item you are selling, and a clear, concise title and description.

Prior to listing your items on an auction site, do some market research to determine if anyone else is selling the same thing. If there is competition, find out details such as how many have sold (look at completed auctions), and what the high bid price was at the end of the auction.

Also, check to see how many people looked at the auction by finding out if there was a "hit counter" added to the listing. These counters usually look like odometers, and are typically located near the bottom of a listing description. Check your auction site's help section for more about how to add counters to your own auctions.

Be creative with your auction titles while being descriptive and relevant. Think about keywords potential buyers may use to find your items. Some auction sites will cancel a listing if they feel that you are "keyword spamming" or using words that are not relevant to the listing. Be aware that using designer names, names of famous people, and misrepresenting your item by using brand names in conjunction with your items may be in violation of copyright restrictions.

Set reserve prices on high-end items. A reserve price is the minimum you will accept for the item you are selling (check seller fees). If the auction bidders bid higher than your reserve price, then you have made money. If not, you will only lose the listing fee and the auction closes without any winning bidders. If you do not set a reserve price, you must accept whatever the highest bid is at the end of the auction.

Be watchful of user feedback and potential scams. Even though systems are in place to prevent fraud, be aware that it does exist and people get tricked all the time.

Auction sites have started a lot of businesses for people who otherwise would have had a difficult time starting out. Once you have a positive feedback rating built up, customers will feel safe about buying from you. You may also see a lot of return customers. If you are doing well selling on auction sites, you may not need a conventional website or "dot-com" to sell your products.

Buying Materials, Equipment & Products For Your Business Using Auctions

Online auctions are a great resource for buying fabrics, tools, equipment, and notions. Do some research and be clear on what your are buying before you bid. Always check a seller's feedback rating and check their shipping policies before you bid.

If you know what you are searching for and know how to use the search tools on auction sites effectively, it should be easy to find lots of great deals. For example, some keywords to use when looking for particular types of fabrics using the search tools on online auction sites are:

> Linen fabric
> Velvet fabric scraps
> Blue brocade fabric
> Fabric lot

Example keywords for machinery:

> Singer Sewing Machine
> New Janome Serger
> Singer 610

Use the minus sign "-" in front of words to omit them if you are getting too many things you do not want. For example, if you keep getting too many "silk fabric dresses" when all you want to see is silk fabric, type "silk fabric -dresses" in the search box. The term NIB (new in box), NWT (new with tags) or NEW will find new items.

Be careful when buying from sellers located overseas as you could be subject to paying import taxes as well as other charges when your shipment arrives in the United States. It is illegal for someone to ship you items from overseas without declaring the shipment's true value.

Also, many people try to label items as "gift" and if the customs inspector finds otherwise, both the shipper and recipient can be fined and held accountable. As well as these legal caveats, remember the quality may not be what you are expecting.

Do thorough research before you bid. The auction may seem like a good deal at the time, but when you factor in shipping and handling costs, plus time to ship, think about whether it would be a better deal to buy locally, if available. If you are looking for equipment, check the item description for "refurbished" or "factory second" and reconsider the quality and potential problems.

Check other auction sites and websites throughout the internet and compare prices. Read the manufacturer's description if you are looking to buy equipment (www.epinions.com), as well as product reviews as necessary. Make sure that you are clear on model numbers, as sometimes sellers do not list them. The bottom line: Know what you are buying.

Never bid on something unless you are sure you want it and are willing to pay for it. Backing out of an auction is bad business practice, and in most cases will earn you negative feedback. In some cases, the seller will lose listing fees. Most auction sites will tell you that bidding is the same as entering into a contract with the seller.

There are several books out on the market that will tell you how to get the best deals on online auctions, how to "snipe" or steal a deal at the last second, and what to expect when buying and selling using auctions. Research will pay off!

Further Reading:

Internet Auctions for Dummies, by Greg Holden, ISBN 0764505785

Starting an eBay Business for Dummies, by Marsha Collier, ISBN 0764569244

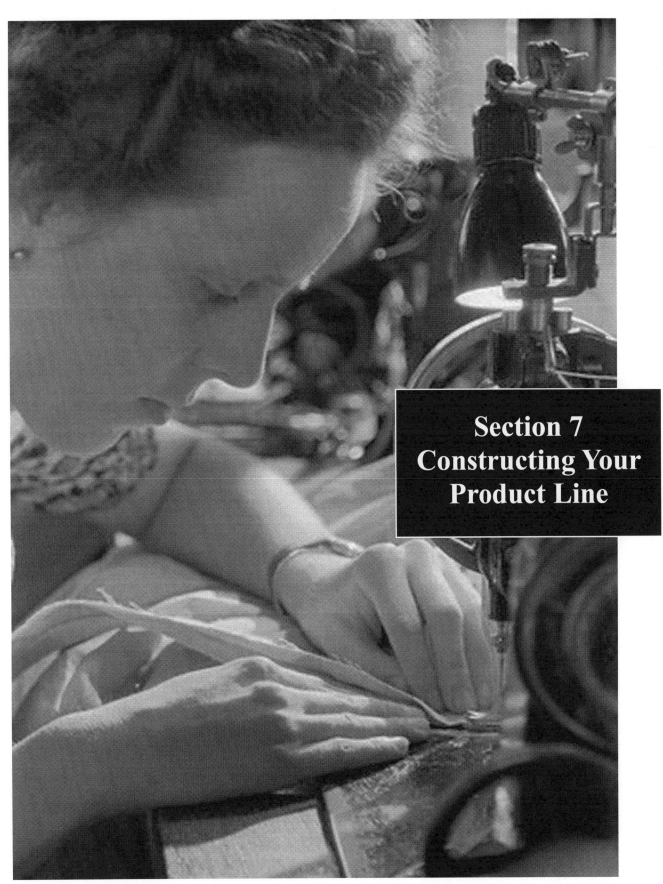

**Section 7
Constructing Your
Product Line**

The Designs

For whatever you will be sewing, you will need a basic draft, pattern, or sketch of the design. For example, if you are making dolls, you will need sketches of the final design, and some sturdy pattern templates that you can use repeatedly to cut out the pieces from your fabric.

If you have purchased patterns, check the copyright restrictions on commercial use. Many pattern companies will not allow mass production of their designs (see Section 11, Copyrights & Intellectual Property). Some pattern companies will allow you to purchase rights, but this can be expensive. It is better to create your own designs and patterns.

Pattern design software is a good tool when you are creating designs. Most programs do not require a great deal of computer knowledge, and the clothing patterns that are produced usually provide a good fit.

After you have created a prototype of your design, and identified any areas that need improvement, you are ready to purchase supplies and mass produce your line.

You might decide to produce items as they are ordered, or stock certain items, sizes and colors, so that when an order comes in, all you have to do is pick the item, package it and ship it out to the customer. Consider that whichever method of production and inventory storage that you choose will affect your taxes.

If you are creating your own nationally branded item, eventually, you may be contracting out services to a manufacturing company. You can rely on employees, family and friends to help with the manufacturing process if your operation is at home or on a smaller scale.

Your Work Area

Designate an area to work—preferably that is used only for work. If you must use your kitchen table, the less clutter around your work the better. Make sure your work surface is clean and free of food or liquids.

Layout, cutting, and assembly can be a tedious process. Rather than working on one item at a time, cut out all of your designs and assemble in "assembly line" style, and then sew to save time.

Storage Area

Have a storage area set aside for materials, finished products, and shipping materials. Keep inventory and supplies separate from things you may use at home.

Other Key Points:
- Set and stick to regular work hours
- Set a realistic budget for business expenses and stick to it
- Create impressive packaging for your products, using your logo and other clean, new packaging materials
- After each project or run of production, make sure all of your equipment is left in good order for the next time you need it

**Section 8
Photographing &
Displaying
Your Product Line**

PHOTOGRAPHY

Displaying & Photography of Your Products

Professional Photography
Hiring a professional photographer will give you the best photograph quality, display, and light. Professional photographers work either by the hour, or flat rate for photo sessions. Some reasons why people do not typically use professional photographers when starting out are cost and copyright.

When a professional photographer photographs your products, they use top of the line equipment, lighting and resources. Once you pick the images from the portfolio of photographs taken at the session, you pay for the prints. The professional photographer holds the copyright to the images, and you must have written consent to reproduce them. For example, you cannot go down to your local 1-hour photo for copies of a photo taken by a professional photographer. Usually, photographers stamp the back of a photo with their copyright information, and most places will not copy a photo with this stamp unless it comes with consent.

Clothing
When photographing clothing, to make the clothing "come alive," you will need a model. You could photograph the product on a nice dress form, but the characteristics and drape of the fabric and article of clothing is best displayed when worn by a person.

Hiring a professional model can be expensive, but if it is just a one-time project, then the investment may be worth it. Be prepared to pay the model for travel expenses, makeup, hair styling, shoes, and their time. Depending upon the model's experience and popularity, expect to pay at least $75 per hour for their time.

You could also photograph the garments on yourself or someone in your family or circle of friends. Be picky about who best represents the product, and think of the look you want to convey to your potential customers.

Doing it Yourself: Digital Cameras
Purchase a high-quality digital camera and photo editing software to create quality images for your website and portfolio on your own. Use a light box, or a good quality photography light, backdrops, and a tripod to create the best pictures.

Backdrops
100-yard rolls of muslin fabric can be purchased for about $100 (see Appendix for suppliers). Designs can be hand painted or airbrushed on to create a backdrop for your photography. Backdrops that are ready to use can be purchased through a photography store or auction site, usually under $500.

Whatever method you decide to use when photographing and displaying your products, make sure it best represents the look you want. Do not settle for a method just because you do not have a lot of money to spend— find a way to get it done right. Think of photography as an investment and one of the best ways in which you can represent your product line.

**Section 9
Quality Control**

QUALITY

During the process of manufacturing your product line, take some time to double check your work before it gets sent out to your customers. A little time spent checking for quality will insure that your customers are happy.

Take some time to examine your competitor's products. You may see little things that bring down the level of quality of the product, especially if it is mass-produced. It could be a few strings dangling that were not cut from a serger, or seams that are coming apart because they were not stitched securely.

This type of sloppiness is exactly what you do not want your customers to see in your products. Examine your products and look for "loose ends" to tie up.

Check for tears, cuts you may have missed, or crooked stitching. For garments, check all stress points for secure stitching, wrinkles, and uneven seams. Make the inside of the garment look as good as the outside. Check the tension on your machine to make sure it is set up correctly to prevent problems. Always make sure that you are using the correct needle and thread size for the fabric you are sewing.

When you purchase fabric, check it for stains, slubs, missing threads, or any other defect before preshrinking or cutting.

Your work represents you and your business. If you are having other people do the sewing for you, follow up and check the quality.

Create customer satisfaction cards and include them with each shipment, or create a form online that customers can use to give you feedback.

Use the Quality Control Checklist on the following page to decide on what standards you will have for checking your products. Make it part of the construction process to check each item for quality.

Consider including these items on your surveys to customers:

◊ What was your overall rating of this product?
◊ Would you recommend this product to someone else?
◊ What could be done to improve this product?
◊ Would you buy this product again?
◊ Was your order handled promptly?
◊ Were you happy with the customer service that you received during this transaction?

Quality Control Checklist

✓ Are you using the proper stitch selection for your machine and the fabric being used?

✓ Does the finished design look like your product pictures your customers see?

✓ If you are sewing lettering, is the spelling/grammar correct?

✓ Is the lettering type clear and easily readable?

✓ Are you using the correct color of thread for your fabric?

✓ Is the finished size of the product correct?

✓ Is the product top heavy or lopsided in appearance? (stuffing, proportions, etc.)

✓ Are the measurements correct?

✓ If applicable, has the correct backing or interfacing been selected?

✓ Are there any toppings or facings required?

✓ Have the correct needle and thread types and sizes been selected?

✓ Is your machine working properly?

✓ Are there threads hanging loose on the finished product?

✓ Are the seams sturdy?

✓ Does the stitch balance look consistent on the design?

✓ Are machine thread tensions adjusted consistently?

✓ If embroidering, was the embroidery pattern aligned and positioned properly on the sewn product?

✓ Are all points and corners finished properly?

✓ Are any parts of the product too bulky or thick?

✓ Are there any threads that were not trimmed properly?

✓ Are there any missed stitches due to thread breakage that need to be repaired?

✓ Are stitches formed properly (not too loose or too tight)?

✓ Signs of looping or malformed stitches?

✓ Are the seams pressed flat?

✓ Is the bobbin thread seen on topside of embroidery?

✓ Is there any damage to the fabric caused by the needle size or too many stitches sewn in the same area?

✓ Is there excessive puckering, wrinkles or drawing up of fabric or thread?

✓ For embroidery, are there excessive hoop marks that need to be steamed away?

✓ Is the fabric damaged in anyway? (cuts, marks, stains, etc.)

✓ If trim or binding has been added, is it straight?

✓ Does the appearance of the product overall have a neat, well finished look?

**Section 10
Finance**

FINANCE

Most sewing businesses can be started without financing, on a shoestring budget. Having the necessary equipment on  hand before starting the business will save investment money. Look around your sewing room – do you already own a sewing machine? Do you have fabric stashed away in a closet that could be making money for you?

You could finance everything, or use your personal credit cards, and pay back the debt as you go, though this will increase risk to your personal credit. If you decide to finance your business, make sure you have a back up source of income until your business becomes stable. If it is not necessary to go into debt, avoid it.

Invest in up-to-date bookkeeping software. This will help you track your assets, inventory and sales, as well as bills and expenses. It is important that you keep track of your bookkeeping at all times, regardless of whether or not you have hired an accountant. If you do not know exactly what you are spending, you could be losing money.

After completing your business plan, you should have a clear idea of what your resources and liabilities will be. If you update it often, you should be able to see a noted increase in both profit and experience.

Hire a bookkeeper and/or tax consultant for help with estimated taxes, social security and investment programs. It is tempting, after your business starts successfully, to pocket all of your profits. If you are serious about staying in business, you need to review your personal finances and make sure you are not living off all of your business income. This is a guaranteed way of running your business into the ground.

Pay yourself a living wage, but remember that profits over and above what you charge for labor should be reinvested to help your business grow. Any profit made by your business should pay debt incurred, or reinvested for future inventory or equipment purchases. If there is not anything left after paying your regular expenses, then you need to work harder, reconsider your pricing and expenditures, or re-think your product line and marketing strategies.

Accepting Credit Cards
Most people that have a reasonably good credit history can set up merchant accounts without problem. It is possible, though more expensive, to set up a merchant account if you do not have a good credit rating. Obtain a copy of your credit report and research the internet for merchant account and credit card processors.

If a processor or agent feels that your business is high-risk, possibly fraudulent, or that your credit history is extremely unstable, they may decline your application.

When searching for a credit card processing company, beware of fraud and identity theft scams, and stick to reputable companies that have up-front contact information, easy to understand policies, and are well established.

Check with your local bank to find out what services they may be able to offer you. Some banks have restrictions on the type of account you must open in order to accept credit cards. They may decline your application if you are not credit-worthy, or have not been a long-term customer in good standing.

If for some reason you cannot use your own local bank to process credit cards, you will need to find a merchant account agent.

Once the risk level of your business venture and credit history are considered, and your application has been approved, the agent will then put you in touch with a payment processor, who will assign merchant ID numbers (they look like credit card numbers) to your business.

Both the agent and processor will get a small portion of your sales, and will likely charge a monthly fee of around $10-$45. These fees may vary by processor and agent, but should be explained when you sign up for your account.

In addition, you will need to set up a secure website (SSL), as well as shopping cart software or payment "gateway" in order for customers to enter their credit card information (see Section 12, Your Website) during a transaction. You can opt to collect your customer's credit card number over the phone and then manually enter this information into your payment processor's secure website.

After a transaction, you will get an e-mail receipt. Usually, funds are deposited into your business bank account within a few days, less the transaction fee, which is usually 1-5%. There may be processes that you are required to complete at the end of each business day, such as batch processing your total sales. Find out the requirements for these functions from your processor or agent.

Keep in mind that if you cancel a merchant account contract (for example if you do not want to accept credit cards through a particular agent, or go out of business) before your contract is expired, you may have to pay a fee to the agent, and breaking a contract can be expensive. Make sure to read all of your contracts before agreeing to anything.

If you have a retail store, the processing company agent will arrange to set up a system for processing transactions, usually electronically or with an imprinter. Transaction printers can be expensive to lease, so research equipment pricing options before committing to a lease.

The agent will also ask which credit cards that you would like to accept. Do not feel like you must accept all forms of credit cards. Each company (Visa® , Mastercard®, American Express®, and Discover®) all have their own fee structures, membership fees, and restrictions that are not included in agent and processor agreements.

Research all contracts, restrictions, and options before signing any legally binding financial agreement, and know your legal rights for cancelling a contract. Compare merchant agents pricing structures and rules before making your final decision.

Once you are approved to accept credit cards, obtain the credit card company logos to advertise which cards you accept. If you have set up a physical storefront, the credit card companies will send you stickers and logo artwork directly, as well as processing forms and other supplies, which you will reorder through them. You can download credit card logos from card company websites and apply them to your website once you have an approved merchant account.

If you are selling merchandise using auctions, you may want to open a business account through an online company such as PayPal, or Western Union's BidPay. These accounts are easy to open and will be invaluable when you need to receive payments from customers. These types of accounts may be used outside of auction sales. Considering the cost of a credit card transaction through a merchant agent, these companies are inexpensive.

Their fees are competitive with merchant agents, and you do not have to have a sparkling credit history or jump through any hoops to open an account. With PayPal, funds can be deposited into your checking account, or you can carry a credit balance for online purchases you may make. In addition to online accounts, PayPal and Western Union both offer debit cards.

Research processing companies and be clear on their policies and spending restrictions. They all have limitations to protect customers from fraud, such as setting new member spending limits and verifying personal information.

Also, if there is reason to believe there is fraudulent activity relating to deposits or withdrawals from your account, they have the right to freeze funds in your account until they can sort out the situation, whether it is

your fault or not. This practice has earned some companies bad reputations, but it is a necessary function of the banking industry to protect people from fraud.

For whichever method you choose to accept credit cards for your business, beware of fraudulent e-mails or telephone calls regarding your account. There have been millions of messages e-mailed to account holders from outside sources that look like legitimate messages. This is called "phishing."

These messages come with all the graphics and live links to the legitimate company websites, but they also include links that redirect you to a fraudulent website in order to collect personal information about you.

An example of a fraudulent e-mail sent to a PayPal customer included all of PayPal's graphics, and several links to their policy web pages, but also included a link to a personal website that directed respondents to enter their passwords and social security numbers. A legitimate company would never ask for this information.

See the article on "phishing" at www.webopedia.com/TERM/p/phishing.html for more information.

Always check the URL or website address of a link sent to you in any e-mail correspondence you may receive. Do not click the link to visit the website; right-click over the link to see its URL/web address.

For more help with Business Finance:

Entrepreneur Magazine
www.entrepreneur.com

Home Business Magazine
Available through Amazon.com
ASIN B00005N7QS

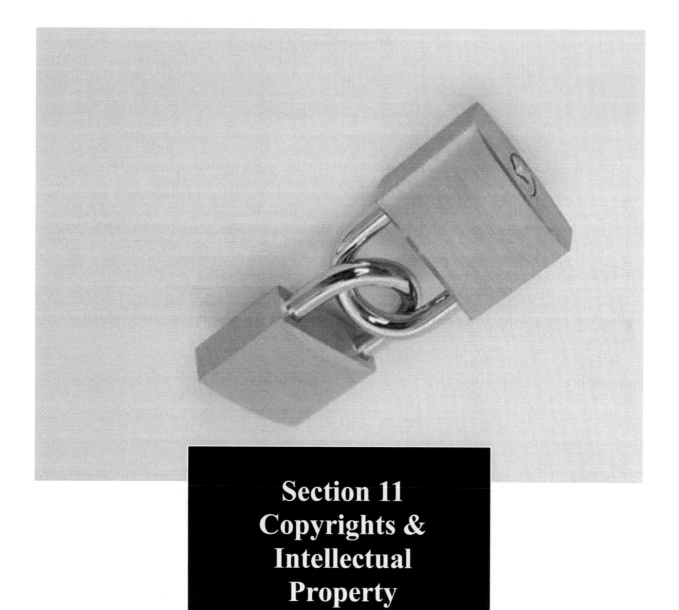

Section 11
Copyrights &
Intellectual
Property

Here are some rules to remember when promoting your business, designing products, creating an advertising campaign or developing your website.

Never take images from a website without written permission from the owner.
This includes research, pictures, backgrounds on web pages, icons, drawings, and other special graphics. The owner of the website could sue you for copyright infringement.

It is unethical to use other people's artwork and design ideas. It could impact your business in a seriously negative way and result in a messy lawsuit if you post a design and the original designer sees your posting. Business owners (and customers) in the sewing industry watch out for each other, and if they see a copyright infringement, they will act upon it quickly. Do not risk your business or your reputation; use your own pictures.

Never copy someone else's research or work into your website and call it your own work.
This is called plagiarism. Always cite your sources, and always do your own work.

Never use pattern company pictures as examples of designs on your website, or sell a design as your own design after using a pattern company's pattern.
There has been some debate over the years as to whether or not someone could sell items based on a pattern company's design. Some people say that to sell an item based on a pat-

tern design, the person copying the design has to change the design substantially to be within legal rights, or that the person may only sell their labor and not the pattern (but you cannot use the company's pictures from the pattern envelopes or catalogs to promote the products). Here is letter from Simplicity Pattern Company about this issue:

"Patterns are considered printed matter, and are covered under copyright laws. Treat them just like you would books or videos — you can share them with anyone but once you start making copies, and especially if you are selling those copies, you are clearly violating the rights of the author/designer.

If you are sewing as a seamstress, the legal interpretation is that the customer requesting the garment owns the pattern, and you are only selling your work or skills as a seamstress.

If you are sewing products in mass production, for the retail or wholesale market, no matter how small the volume, you are selling the design — which in this case belongs to Simplicity. You would therefore, be in clear violation of the copyright laws, and subject to legal action."

Advice? Obtain written permission from the company who owns the copyright of the pattern you would like to use. To be safest, draft your own patterns and designs.

Never put logos from other companies on your website without written consent, even if you are promoting them.
Obtain written permission from a company owner before you advertise or promote them. If you do not gain consent, then you are using their trademark without permission. You may see nothing wrong with promoting another business, but are you sure they want *you* to promote them? It is always best to ask first.

Always give credit if you are given permission to use something for your website.
If you do gain consent for use of items that are not yours, make sure you give credit where credit is due by citing your sources, and make a note that permission was granted for limited rights.

Protect your own designs
To show customers your products, create a professional-quality website or portfolio that has high resolution pictures of each item in your product line. You may need to enlist a model to display your creation, and you may also have to hire a professional photographer to get the best results. Both the model and the photographer can be expensive, but usually the expense will be worth the results.

It is very disconcerting to find that another person has copied your pictures (which you may have paid for) onto their website, or even into their portfolio to call their own.

A professional photographer copyrights pictures that they have taken, so even though the picture may be yours to display, the work is still covered by the photographer's own copyright. When displaying a photographer's work, remember to give them credit by listing their name by the photo or on a special cred-

its page within your website. Check display restrictions and royalty requirements if you use a professional photographer or model for your photographs.

Protect your pictures if you post them to your website by following these tips:

Use a watermark
Using graphics software, create a copy of your logo or business name, then make it semi-transparent, with a light drop-shadowed edge. Place this "watermark" over your image to be protected. Do not place the watermark in a corner of the picture; make it transparent enough to see through and put it directly over the main part of the picture. This way, when you post a picture, if someone copies it, it will bear your name and logo, and will be difficult for someone to edit out.

Use special scripts
Use special "scripts" to create a picture gallery for displaying your designs on your website. This can make your website trickier to design, build and edit, but makes it harder for thieves to copy an image if it is published in this manner. Protect the directories of your website by hiding and password protecting them.

Do not send unprotected copies of your work to anyone
If you create custom designs, or offer designs not listed within your product catalog, people may want to see other examples of your work. Place a watermark over any pictures you distribute, or post a scripted gallery web page (image directories hidden) with your images for the customer to view, without being able to copy or print the images.

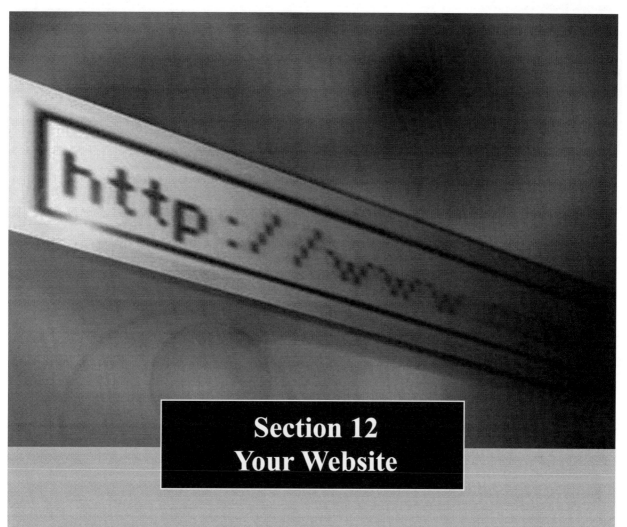

Section 12
Your Website

Nowadays, building a website may be the most important thing you do for your business—it is less expensive than opening a traditional brick-and-mortar business, has low overhead costs, and it is the best way to get the word out about your sewing business.

WEBSITE

If you would like to build your own website but you have limited computer or web page building knowledge, enroll in a community college course on web page building. It is worth the expense, and if you can gain the basic understanding of how a page is put together and what makes it work, you will save yourself a lot of time and money in the long run. You will not have to rely on a design professional every time you want to make a change to your website, such as adding a new item or adjusting pricing.

Building a Web Page On Your Own
If you plan on building your website on your own, acquire a copy of a page editor such as Microsoft FrontPage™ or Macromedia's Dreamweaver™.

If you have a local Internet Service Provider (ISP), they should be able to offer the following services. Do thorough research and compare provider packages to find the best prices.

Register a domain name for your website. In essence, this will be a "dot-com" (or dot-net, dot-org, etc). You can incorporate your business name into this, for example, if your business name is Mary's Creations, then you could use www.maryscreations.com, if the domain name was available. If the name is not available, then go back to name clustering for other variations as you might have done when originally naming your business.

There are many websites on the internet that will register a domain name for you. Do thorough research before you decide on one place to purchase your domain name.

Next, find a host for your website. A host is a provider who will store all of your website's files on their servers. There are many companies that advertise website hosting, as well as domain registration and hosting packages. Some are free, but you may have pop-up ads as with GeoCities or FreeWebs, which can be annoying to viewers.

Check with your website host to find out about their schedule for server maintenance and how often they back up their customer websites. Keep a copy of your website on a CD, DVD, or on a secure hard drive as your own safe backup.

Set up any e-mail accounts that you would like to associate with your business. Your website host will have instructions for how to do this, or you may be able to have them set up your e-mail accounts as you need them.

Once your website is complete, you will know how large it is, including pictures. The host will need to know the size of your website to gauge how much to charge for space.

Your host will also charge you for bandwidth, also called traffic. The more people who access your website, download files and images, the more you will be charged for using up internet bandwidth. Find out the specifics for bandwidth charges and allotments from your hosting company.

To start building your website, you will need a concept of how you want it to look and act. Map your pages out on paper. Look at several websites on the web, not only your competitor's websites, but other commerce websites you may have visited in the past. Has your system crashed at certain websites? What colors and graphics strike you? Do you want a shopping cart? These elements will all affect your potential customer's decision to visit your website again. Keep in mind the viewer's download times, and keep graphics to a minimum. Microsoft FrontPage will show you the download times as you edit.

Viewers should have an easy time navigating your website. It should not look cluttered or too busy, or too plain.   To save your visitor's time, include a sitemap to your website that lists, in text links, ways to navigate around the entire website. Also, develop an easy to understand navigational structure that is consistent throughout the website.

Many web designers are getting away from using frames on websites, and they are using tables. Tables work well with most browsers, and they can also keep their size more consistent than traditional frames. Frames tend to look amateurish, and if you look at many commercial websites, you will see tables are used rather than frames.

As your website grows, it could become tedious updating all of your pages. You need to make sure links to other websites placed on your pages stay as current as possible; check them often. There is software available that will do this for you automatically, or you can sign up for a web check that provides this valuable service over the web.

The more links you have on your website, the more work it will be to maintain them unless you use special style sheets and templates (cascading style sheets – CSS for short),

which can be more complicated to use if you are not familiar with advanced web design. A style sheet is a template that is used to make global changes throughout a website and will save editing time.

Do not place pictures to your entire product line on one page. Break up and organize items into different pages, and use thumbnails where you can. Keep in mind that interactive buttons increase download time, just the same as images. Place links around your website at the bottom or down the side of each page so that viewers can navigate easily.

Include a legal page. You will need one if you accept credit cards. The legal page is a good place to put your copyright information, website rules, and your refund/return policy. See the Appendix section for a sample.

You may also want to include a page of resources that you enjoy, such as books, periodicals, art, movies and music. Amazon.com is one of many companies that offers an affiliate program for books and media. Commissions are made by customer referrals to their website. Research other commission opportunities such as banner ads from other websites to generate affiliate income. Google AdSense offers ads that are non-intrusive, are free to use, and will earn commissions with each click.

The fonts and page backgrounds of your website should not interfere with text. Keep the body text of your website uniform, and hard-code the size to 11pt or 12pt. Some browsers are set to size text larger or smaller, and this can ruin the look of your web pages if the size is not hard-coded into the HTML.

When choosing fonts for your website, remember that most people's web browsers are set for basic fonts. If you really want to use fancy fonts, include them as small graphics.

Color coordination of text, graphics, and background images is essential. If your background image does not have anything to do with what you are selling, or is too busy, it shows a lack of taste and professionalism. Many websites do not use backgrounds as they can slow the download speed of a webpage, and can interfere with text.

Your graphics should be 1k to 75k each, clean and sharp, and keep them to less than six per page. Otherwise, if your customers have slow internet connections, it could be tiresome waiting for everything to download, and they could move on to another website.

Place low-resolution thumbnail pictures on your pages, and make them link to a larger picture file (Microsoft FrontPage will do this automatically). This way, if a customer wants to view a graphic, they have the choice to click on a thumbnail and not have to worry about a long download time.

Develop content relevant to your product line. Having articles, product information, informational pages, and stories relating to your products will help search engines rank your website accordingly. The more relevant content you have, the better your chances of a higher ranking.

If you accept credit cards, you will need to find a processor (see Section 10, Finance), and a secure connection for customers to enter their data securely. Your host should be able to recommend processors, and may even market shopping cart software that works best with their servers.

Consider using a payment processor such as PayPal if you have an account. Code for shopping cart buttons for your products can be generated on PayPal's website. With this feature, you do not need a secure payment gateway, and this will save you money on

hosting services as well as time integrating shopping cart software.

Do thorough research when selecting shopping cart software. Some software companies charge a monthly fee to use, and others charge a large one-time fee. Some website hosts will only allow you access to a limited number of shopping cart software options, and this may prevent you from setting up your virtual store the way you want. Keep this in mind when you shop for a host.

What to Expect When Hiring a Consultant to Build Your Website
It may save you money in the long run if you can create your web page on your own. However, if lack of time to learn something new is a factor, or if you are just not into web design, then obtain help from a web page design professional. Make sure that you are ready with your website design plans mapped out on paper and have a clear idea of what you want. This will save time when you meet for your initial consultation with the designer.

The designer should have a portfolio of websites that they have authored, with their business name published somewhere in the website credits, a good reputation, as well as references that you may contact.

The designer should have some templates set up for you to review. If you would like a shopping cart or other special interactive features on your website, make sure the designer knows this in advance.

Expect to pay a web page design professional $80 or more per hour of service. Some will design a website for a flat rate, rather than by the hour. Also, ask about what type of technical support is available, training for you to be able to edit your own pages, and how updates to your website pages will be handled.

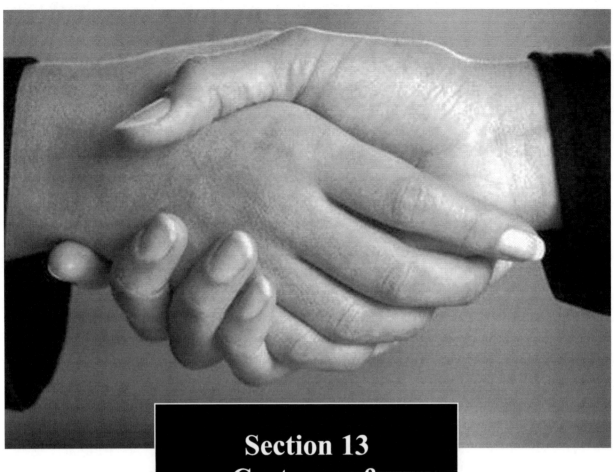

**Section 13
Customer &
Vendor
Relations**

RELATIONS

Dealing With People Everyday in Business

Customer Service

If you run your business primarily over the internet, your direct contact with customers will be relatively low. The only time you will need to speak with customers directly is if they have specific questions, or feel safer calling you with their credit card information rather than using your website.

Check Your Mood At the Door...

In each correspondence, try to keep the mood positive. Always thank the person for writing or calling, and offer further assistance in the future. E-mail the customer regular updates if the merchandise they purchased is taking longer than what you expected, and let them know when their order has shipped, thanking them for their business at the same time.

Even after a long day of work, you still need to address customers in a positive way, realizing that they may not have had the same kind of day you have had. Watch your tone when corresponding; people may read something negative into the conversation based on your mood. Even if the customer asks a question that you may think is a stupid question, you need to address them in a friendly manner, and try to guide the customer. Keep in mind that they may be asking a silly question, but later they could become a repeat customer or refer more business to you.

Get Educated

Take a customer service course or seminar if you can afford one, or search for a video recording of a seminar at your local library.

Read some books and articles from periodicals about personality types, and good customer service skills. If you have employees or business partners that have direct contact with customers, put them through some sort of customer service training—even if they are family members or friends.

Network

Your ultimate goal should be to concentrate on making a positive name for yourself and your business in the industry. Get to know some of the other people in the sewing industry through e-lists or other networks, even though they may be your competition. There is so much work to go around in this business, and you will find that having some reliable sewing resource contacts will be helpful.

The Customer is Always Right

If you want the sale, remember the customer is always right, so if they are dead set on something you would never want for yourself, and you have given them your best, educated opinion of it, you need to go with what the customer wants. If you are not interested in working with the customer on something that may be questionable, be up-front with them and gracefully decline.

Recommended Resources:
Give 'em the Pickle & They'll Be Back
by Bob Farrell & Bill Perkins;
ISBN 1880692333

VHS: Fred Pryor Seminars - How to Handle
Difficult People; ASIN: B0002XTY7A

Vendor Relations

Vendors are also called suppliers. They are businesses and individuals that will sell you products and materials for your business or personal use. Vendors are people that can make your life easier as a business owner. Since they are selling to you, the tables are turned a bit. They are out to get and keep your business.

Think about your favorite vendors. What do they do that you could be doing for your customers? What would you do differently?

Invoices & Payment Terms

Many larger companies will offer to bill you for products that you purchase from them. If your credit is good, or you have solid trade references for your business, they will likely extend credit to you. Read over any terms before you accept credit from vendors. Credit from vendors can be just like debt with credit card companies, and is just as costly.

Many vendors offer special billing terms. For example, if you pay the invoice completely before the due date, you will receive a discount. You may see things on your bill such as "2% 10 Net 30", which means you will receive a 2% discount if you pay the net of the invoice within 10 days. They expect the whole of the bill paid within 30 days. Net means the subtotal without shipping and handling fees or taxes.

Receiving Items

Have a process in order to keep things moving smoothly when you receive orders. You may be swamped with customer orders, be busy with phone calls, or other problems, and then a huge delivery truck pulls into your driveway with a shipment you forgot you ordered.

Keep track of things you order by adding them to your organizer calendar or portable day planner (see Section 17, Staying Organized). Have people ready to help with your incoming shipment if necessary; some delivery companies will not carry heavy products into your business.

Have your copy of your order with you when the shipment arrives. If your vendor agreement states that any shipment you sign for cannot be returned, this means you will need to inspect the shipment before you sign for and accept it.

Look for damaged items, and match the items against your copy of the order to make sure the order has been filled correctly. This process is time consuming and many freight delivery companies do not like to take the extra time for inspections of deliveries. Insist upon inspection if you have this type of agreement with your vendor.

Returns to Your Vendor

If you do need to return an item, and your vendor accepts them for a refund or exchange, be very clear about their return process. The vendor may require you to pay for shipping, insurance, and tracking back to them. They may also require an RA# (return authorization number) to be clearly written on the outside of the shipping container before they will accept a return. Most vendors will not accept responsibility for damaged shipments.

Favorite Vendors

Keep a contact list of your favorite vendors handy so that it is easy to place orders when needed. Include the vendor's phone number, address, time zone, sales representative name, and your account or customer number if applicable. Have your orders repeated to you to insure accuracy of the entry into the vendor's order system. Also, be clear on shipping and handling fees, delivery dates, tracking IDs, shipping methods, and taxes.

**Section 14
Packaging &
Shipping**

SHIPPING

Presentation Is Everything

Packaging is part of customer service

When a customer receives a package from you, they should feel like it is Christmas or their birthday. Make sure things are neat, and add extra promotional items as gifts, and as an example of your good customer service.

When packaging items for shipment, always use a new, sturdy box, without holes, markings, or handle cuts, large enough to ship what you are sending out. An item crumpled and stuffed in a tiny, ill-fitting or soiled box is not the best representation of your products and services.

Wrap clothing in plastic garment bags. These can be obtained from some dry cleaners or a packaging warehouse in several sizes (www.uline.com). They are sold as a perforated roll in a few different lengths. Using these bags will keep moisture and potential shipping spillages away from your products.

Choose a non-printed paper for wrapping the order, and lining the box. Crumple the paper if you need filler to keep items from shifting. U-haul sells an inexpensive recycled plain paper for wrapping items. Do not use packing peanuts. Many people are annoyed by the sight of packing peanuts, and they stick to fabric.

Use a good quality shipping label, and either type or word process a label so that the address information is clear. Research ways you can print labels and postage online. The United States Post Office (USPS) has a pro-gram called Click-N-Ship®, and provides free delivery confirmation with most shipments. You can also request packages to be picked up, so you can bypass the lines at the post office. Also, check out Stamps.com for printable postage options.

If you ship out of the country, you will need to include customs forms. Be honest on these forms about the value of the product. The customs fees are the responsibility of the customer, and you should make this clear to them prior to accepting their order and funds. It is illegal to falsify information on the customs forms and has some serious implications.

When shipping a package, always insure it for the full amount the customer paid. Get a delivery confirmation so that you can track the item if needed.

Develop shipping rate sheets for yourself and customers. To estimate shipping costs and delivery times, visit your shipper's web page. To determine accurate shipping weights of packages, purchase an inexpensive digital scale at your local office supply store or online auction for less than $40.

Never charge customers an obvious handling fee. Overhead costs such as boxes, paper and tape, should be worked into your merchandise prices. Customers will appreciate not being charged extra fees. If you use USPS to ship items, they offer some shipping supplies for free.

**Section 15
Refunds &
Returns**

Have a refund and return policy in place for your business. A refund and return policy protects both you and your customers, and provides your customers with a stronger sense of trustworthiness, and it may be required by your bank if you accept credit cards.

Some businesses charge a restocking fee to take back an item, depending on the customer's reason for return of the item. It is a good idea to offer to fix any problems with a returned item free of charge. Hopefully, your refund and return policy will discourage customers from returning used goods. When there is a problem with an item, many customers are happy if the business offers to make repairs or replacement.

Be clear on what you will do for your customers. If the problem with the item is the customer's fault, such as incorrect measurements for custom work, it is ethical to charge the customer a fee to repair or replace the item, plus shipping.

For custom clothing, make sure that you have documentation, such as the customer's original measurements, as a back up in case there is any argument. Also, ask for a professional to measure the customer if there are questions of measuring accuracy. If the error is yours, admit to it, apologize, and fix the error quickly.

Sometimes, arguing with a customer over a return is not worth the trouble and risk to

your reputation. Even if you are positive the customer was at fault, consider the situation carefully and weigh your options. Try to do what is best for your business before charging the customer or disputing an issue.

Here is a sample policy sent to us from a clothier on the internet:

"We gladly accept unused merchandise that bears no sign of wear or damage and that has all original tags attached.

Customers must obtain a return authorization number (RA) before merchandise may be returned. Customers may e-mail us to obtain an RA number. The RA number must be clearly written on the outside of the package, or the package will be not be accepted. We are not responsible for damages that occur after delivery. Shipping costs are paid for by the customer.

There are no returns for any item which is customized for size. If you should decide to return an item, we ask that it be sent back insured for the full value (the amount you paid for the item) via a traceable method (UPS, Federal Express, etc.)

Once we have received the returned garment, we will provide an exchange or issue a store credit. Shipping and handling charges are non-refundable for returned or exchanged items.

Merchandise may be returned for exchange or credit refund within ten business days of the receipt of purchase. Returns will not be accepted after this time. Unauthorized returns will not be accepted under any circumstances, and unmarked parcels (without an RA number) will be returned to the sender."

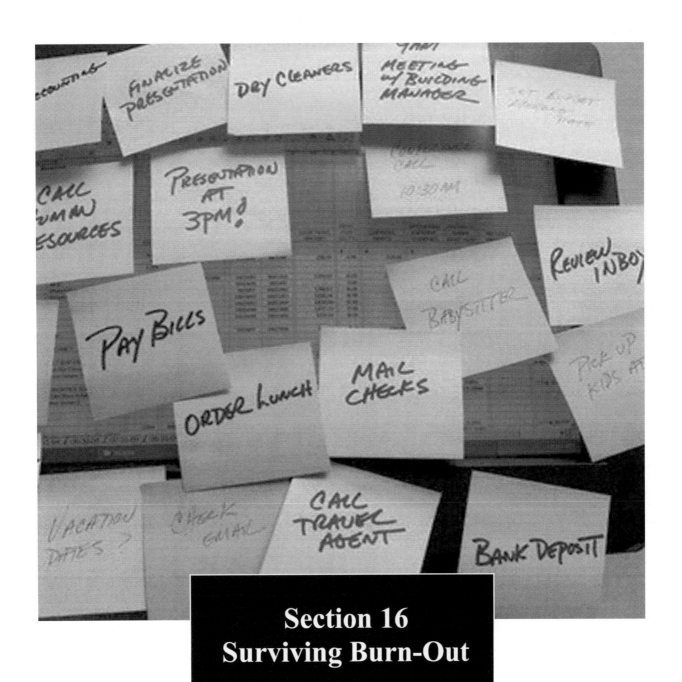

Section 16
Surviving Burn-Out

BURN-OUT

What To Do When You Have Done Too Much

If you are feeling pressured by the responsibilities of business, it is easy to feel unmotivated, or even physically ill. If you find yourself working on projects until two o'clock in the morning for several nights, then having to arise at six o'clock the next day to go to your secure day job, you may find yourself getting behind in your work and feeling physically drained. This is called burn-out and it can be dangerous to your business and to your health.

you may have other customers that are waiting as well—but you will still be responsible for making them feel like a priority.

Set regular work hours that you will sew and stick to them. Take breaks throughout a project, making sure you rest your hands and hydrate yourself. Pick a time during the day (or night) that is uninterrupted, and when you work best. Try to stick to that schedule.

Tips to Avoid Burn-Out

Buy a portable day planner and an erasable wall calendar with erasable pens to keep track of your orders. Space orders out so that you have a break between large projects, and slate time for your own personal projects, if applicable (*remember the saying the cobbler's children never have shoes!*).

Give yourself plenty of time for each project. Be up front with your customers about estimated shipping times before they pay for their order. Do not be irresponsible about promising something to a customer by a certain date, and then not coming through for them, or making it at the last possible minute.

Make sure your customers understand your fulfillment policies and are aware of the timelines involved. Sometimes customers forget

If you are having problems with a project, put it away for a while and come back to it later. Problems have a way of working themselves out if you walk away from them and come back later. Consult newsgroups online for help and ideas from other people who sew.

Find an activity to get your mind off of work for a while. Garden, read, take walks, visit with friends or family, go work out at the gym, or relax in front of a movie to keep your mind off of your project. Do anything that will keep your body active or de-stressed and keep your mind off of work.

Get plenty of sleep on a regular basis. After working too many hours, you will find yourself run down and burned out quickly, which could cause many health problems, and a weaker immune system.

Fitness

Many people who put in a number of hours sewing forget to take a break and exercise. It is easy to be so involved in a project that you can forget to take care of yourself.

In general, you will feel better if you manage your diet and exercise your body, especially if you are out of shape. It does not matter if you need to lose weight; movement and activity will charge your brain and relax your muscles. Sitting over a project for many hours, either at your worktable or in a chair in front of the television, may cause tension in your upper back, headaches, poor circulation, and eyestrain. To prevent or lessen the effects, get moving. Even if you only go for a short walk, move your arms, and enjoy doing something besides sewing. Remember to stay HYDRATED!

Your Eyesight

Ever feel like your eyes have a ton of sand in them while you work? Do you get frequent headaches? Maybe you need to take a break. Eye strain can make you feel tired and stressed. Check to make sure the lighting around your work area is suitable. Get your eyes checked every two years and make sure any lens prescriptions are up to date if you wear glasses or contact lenses.

Overuse Syndrome (Carpel tunnel)

Carpel tunnel is one of the most crippling conditions a person can experience. Anyone that works with their hands would feel depressed and handicapped by this syndrome. Proper stretching, warm up exercises and careful attention to repetitive motion will help deter this condition. Do some research on the internet about this syndrome to find out about the best exercises to prevent it or alleviate pain caused by overuse.

Back problems

Sitting for long periods of time can cause stress on points in your back. If you have ever had a baby, sometimes your tailbone can hurt, simply by sitting for too long. Try yoga, massage, or even simple breathing exercises in addition to taking short walks to loosen your back up and relieve pain.

Edema

Do your legs and feet swell? You may have edema. Contact your doctor immediately if you notice any swelling or water retention.

Obesity

Many hours can go by and you can forget to eat. Or, you may have a non-stop supply of food sitting nearby your work table, and you mindlessly eat, not paying attention to calories or fat. Obesity can lead to many diseases, which we will not go into here, but we thought it was important to bring up the topic as it does relate to your craft. The more inactive you are, the more unhealthy you can become. Get moving and manage your diet. Intentional exercise is an important thing to fit in around your daily life and sewing.

Take care of yourself! Always remember:

You cannot take care of everyone else when you do not take care of your self!

Carve out time for yourself at some point each day; make it uninterrupted time, with no phones, aggravations, or business.

Try meditation, massage, aromatherapy, and candles to help soothe your nerves.

Don't worry about what you look like— worry about your health.

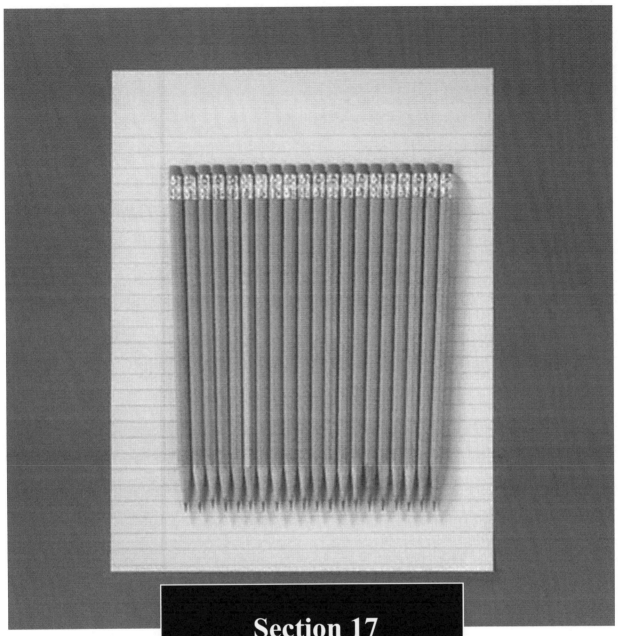

Section 17
Staying Organized

ORGANIZE

There are many ways in which you can stay organized. Some people are just naturally disorganized and have trouble keeping things together. You do not have to be one of them.

Starting with your tools, keep everything in an accessible spot. Use utensil dividers in drawers to separate your hand tools. When you have finished with a tool, train yourself to put it back after each use.

Use shelves and bookcases to your advantage. Stackable bins and sorting trays will keep your paperwork orderly. File your books and periodicals in an order that is easy for you to access what you need when you need it.

Buy racks to sort and organize your thread spools, and mount them on the wall to keep them out of your way while you work.

Buy and label clear plastic bins to store items such as patterns, trims, and notions. This way you can see inside without having to un-stack everything to find something.

Use plastic bead trays to sort small objects such as beads, needles, and other notions. They do not tip easily and will keep things organized.

Move your studio furniture in a way so that it is efficient and ergonomic for you. Use wall mounted shelves to save space. Even if you have limited space, you can make the best use of it by mapping out items on paper, cut-ting out pieces to resemble your furniture (in scale), and figuring out where things will fit.

Use zip ties to bind up wires and cords neatly, and store the bundles out of the way of tripping and out of sight. Make sure your surge protectors and any extension cords are not overloaded, dusty, or unsafe.

Buy a turntable platform (lazy-Susan) to hold jars of pencils, art supplies, or other things you may need to access regularly.

Use crates, shelves, or cube organizers for folded fabrics. Protect your fabrics by cover-ing them with PVC-free plastics or canvas.

Throw out scraps, outdated periodicals, old mail, and other items that you do not need. If you have trouble throwing away periodicals, think about tearing out the pages and articles that interest you and combine them in an arti-cle scrapbook binder for future reference.

Use an empty box for fabric scraps and when it is full, dispose of them if you are not going to use them right away for a project. Many non-profit organizations can benefit from fabric scraps, or you can sell them on an auc-tion site to quilters.

Buy an erasable calendar to help organize your personal responsibilities, vendor ship-ments, and customer deadlines. Try using a portable day planner calendar system to help you remember things on-the-go, keep track of addresses, and organize your responsibilities.

A file cabinet works better than file cases, but work with what you can afford or have on hand. Store stacking trays and bins on top of file cabinets, to best utilize the space on top of them.

Sort out your files in a way that makes sense to you so that you will have quick access to papers when you need them. File customer receipts, your bills, current product catalogs (notice we say *current*!), advertising campaign information, your business plan, résumé, taxes, and any other important business-related documents you may need to access.

Buy a disk storage box for computer software, DVDs, and CDs, where you may have important electronic data files stored.

Use a cabinet or closet with shelving to store office supplies and printer paper, which will keep things safe and away from sun and moisture.

To stabilize your pattern pieces, use iron on interfacing, and store in tubes or flat in sealable bags or file boxes for easy access. Organize by type of pattern or size.

Spend 10 to 15 minutes after each work session cleaning up your workspace. This will save time for the next work session.

Try using a fabric organizer system, such as the one offered at SewOrganized.com. The link to the form is: http://seworganized.com/stashform.html

Create a "Command Central" or a special area for office-related supplies such as pens, pencils, notepads, phone, and other materials. Create a shipping area for your scale, boxes, tape, and other shipping materials.

Sort mail in baskets with labels that indicate action needed to process: to pay, to read, to file, to sign, etc. Throw away anything that you do not need, such as advertisements, as soon as you get them. Set aside time every week to process your written correspondence and phone calls.

Start a "To Do" list, and prioritize your responsibilities. Feel a sense of accomplishment as you work your way down the list, completing tasks. If you have employees or a business partner helping you with your business, assign them a list of responsibilities to distribute the work flow evenly.

Check Out These Resources:

Dream Sewing Spaces: Design & Organization for Spaces Large & Small
by Lynette Black
ISBN 0935278419

Organizing Plain and Simple: A Ready Reference Guide with Hundreds of Solutions to Your Everyday Clutter Challenges
by Donna Smallin
ISBN 1580174485

Organizing for Dummies
by Eileen Roth, Elizabeth Miles
ISBN 0764553003

Organizing for the Creative Person: Right-Brain Styles for Conquering Clutter, Mastering Time, and Reaching Your Goals
by Dorothy Lehmkuhl, and Dolores Cotter Lamping
ISBN 0517881640

Organizing for Success
by Kenneth Zeigler
ISBN 007145778X

**Section 18
Advice From
Successful People in
the Sewing Industry**

ADVICE

Tips From People in the Business

When embarking on a new business venture, it is always a good idea to talk with someone who has been in the business and knows the ropes. Not everyone has access to someone who has succeeded in building a successful sewing business, so we have added some interviews in this section from highly respected people in the industry.

Another good source to tap for information in starting your business are other business-minded people, who have successful small businesses in almost any area of service or manufacturing. The basics are similar from business to business, such as general bookkeeping, building a website, and networking. To find more specialized advice, seek out suppliers, local business people, and members of national organizations, such as the Professional Association of Custom Clothiers (www.paccprofessionals.org).

As with any new business startup, seek legal advice from your attorney, or other legal counsel. It may be wise to consult a financial specialist to determine what your risks to your personal assets will be, especially if you are financing the business using your personal credit, leasing, or buying a studio, or buying expensive equipment. Financial specialists can also help you determine what your tax liability will be, as well offer advice on how to best utilize any profits from your business.

In this section, we have listed interviews from both men and women who started their sewing businesses with little more than their own personal equipment and a high tolerance for risk. They are all highly intelligent, creative people, and are truly inspiring success stories.

Professionals included in this printing are:

Valerie Lilley, Sofi's Stitches, www.sofisstitches.com
Candace Savage, Gypsy Moon, www.gypsymoon.com
Bjarne Drews, Historical Costumes by Bjarne Drews, www.my-drewscostumes.dk
John French, DIY Slipcovers, www.diyslipcovers.com

Valerie Lilley ~ Sofi's Stitches
www.sofisstitches.com

Valerie runs one of the most successful Renaissance costuming businesses on the web. She is popular at Renaissance Faires and her costumes are resold throughout the United States. She started sewing her own line of costumes and the business grew quickly!

How long have you been involved in the costuming industry and what inspired you to start your business?
I've been in the industry for about 10 years. I started Sofi's Stitches in 1997. I don't know what bee got in my bonnet [to start]. I have friends who've been selling their medieval clothes for nearly 13 years now so seeing them might have influenced me a bit. So, I sewed up a dozen outfits and took them to a small event to earn a little extra money on the side and to see what it was like.

How did you start your business—did you start on a shoestring budget?
Oh, yes I started on a shoe string budget! Those first outfits cost $300 in fabric. I already had my sewing machine because designing clothes for my career and for medieval events had been a hobby for years. I didn't even have a clue how to keep proper books, cost analysis or anything. Sofi's Stitches grew so large when I wasn't paying attention that I found I was working two full time jobs. On my 300th dress and it was only September, I decided to either downsize or hire people and go big-time. I went big-time. Small business loan. The works. What made me take the leap? I didn't want to be that 77-year-old woman stitching cute crafts for thrills because she listened to caution while living her life and never started her own clothing company.

If you could offer advice to a person new to the sewing industry, what would it be?
The best advice I got was from the book,

Mother's Work, by Rebecca Mathias. She started her professional maternity clothing company 17 years ago with $10,000. She is now CEO of her publicly traded $300 million company. She said, 'Think big. Focus. Never give up.' I do this all the time. Entrepreneurism is risky all the way. Risk is terribly exciting and exhilarating. Some things you try, and boom, success. Sometimes you try your ideas and they flop. You will make many mistakes. I make mistakes all the time.

How do you survive burn-out?
When a process starts taking up too much time, I analyze it and figure out a more efficient way of doing it. When every process starts taking up too much time, I schedule a 2-3 hours at the end of the day for just me. Then, I take those hours. I fill those hours with things I like to do that has nothing to do with my company. I'm restoring my house, so usually I go work on a house project.

Any other advice?
Learn advertising and marketing. No one knows about you when you first start out. You'll have to spend a goodly percent of gross sales on marketing. Shop your garment district! You'll need to and will become very familiar with your garment district. You will find machines and equipment there. You may find a used one. You may find a better one.

You have to draft patterns and learn to do most things yourself when you first start up. How else are you going to teach employees? You also don't have a ton of money to throw around. You have talent. You can do it yourself.

Start selling your wares on the internet. Teach yourself HTML code writing. It's easy. Try www.webmonkey.com tutorial. I bought my shopping cart from www.MyoBiz.com. Randy the program writer is now like a friend. Get Verisign for secure credit card processing online.

There should be a Small Business Development Center or Small Business Incubator near you. Get their free advice. Take their free seminars. Learn how to use QuickBooks or some other bookkeeping software.

Learn about marketing and advertising because you will do a lot of it. My former career was as a business reporter so I knew some of the business stuff already. My mom is an entrepreneur too, so we talk business on the phone a lot.

The SBA has a mentoring program. Try it. Read books on starting a business on a shoe string budget. Make friends with other clothiers near you who do this for a living. I have several friends who are way bigger than I whom I see at faires and ask questions that come up on the spot. You're not competition for them. I know of one woman who has all her clothes made in Hong Kong and she sews in production runs of 300 dozen per style. All of this seems intimidating when you first start. After your first year, it will all be such a breeze and easy.

Read Valerie's Press Releases on her website at:

http://www.sofisstitches.com/pages/press.shtml

- **2004 Small Business Administration's Business Person of the Year**

- **Sofi's Stitches Inc. and Galerie Hexenhaus Announce Distributorship Agreement**

- **Sofi's Stitches Inc. moves into larger facilities**

- **Call that an anachronism! Internet site offers medieval clothes**

Candace Savage ~ Gypsy Moon
www.gypsymoon.com

Candace has been sewing clothing for over 15 years. She creates lovely wearable art from her studio in Lexington, Massachusetts. She runs an extraordinary clothing business, without a lot of marketing, and is truly an inspirational designer.

What got you started sewing your own line of clothing?
What got me started was making my own dance costumes. I had been collecting antique clothing (and I mean antique, not vintage) for many years and had opened a small business selling Victorian and Edwardian gowns. Some of them fell apart and I saved every scrap I could and then applied the bits as trim to my costumes. So many people stopped me to ask where they could buy them, that I eventually changed my business from antique clothing to modern clothing, using antique styles as inspiration and aging the materials to get the same feel as the antique pieces.

What are the inspirations for the lines you sell? Does the season matter?
The inspiration is the past...faded grandeur. The season does matter, although in the fashion world, the seasons are all mixed up. When civilians are thinking about tweeds and sweaters, we're completely involved in pale chiffons and imagining how things will feel in the dead of summer. We're so out of synch with the actual weather that sometimes I forget that people are looking for something for the holidays...for me it's almost fall again.

Do you draft your own patterns?
We draft all our own patterns.

What couture techniques do you apply?
We do quite a bit of draping and hand sewing, especially for the one-of-a-kind gowns.

Most of our gowns are cut on the bias and because we use such difficult fabrics, they pretty much have to be completely constructed by hand to get them perfect. We also use many of our own techniques for aging and softening fabric and much of it is hand-dyed.

How did you first market your business? I read that people saw what you were wearing and wanted to know where to buy the clothes you had.
I never did market the business, it's been growing by word of mouth.

Where is the clothing line manufactured?
We make everything in Lexington, Massachusetts and that includes our sweaters and knitwear.

What is your personal time investment? It would seem that you sew and design a great deal.
I'm at the studio all day, every day...and sometimes into the night!

What sorts of materials go into your clothing line? I see a lot of silks and velvets; very luxurious!
That's it, silk velvets, silk chiffons, silk jersey, and lots of washed linen for our newest knitwear.

Was it a huge step opening up your store?
It was a huge step opening my dance studio with a tiny shop in the corner. After that, it's been one huge step after another. I wouldn't know what to do with myself if I weren't taking huge steps all the time. It would be so peaceful, I'd probably sit down and never get up again.

Do you have help or support from family members or friends?

My boyfriend, Hans, is very helpful with everything and he has a great eye so I rely on him for feedback. Also, I'm lucky enough to have a beautiful and photogenic daughter who models for me. She has great style and ideas so I always listen to her. Jennifer, the shop manager, is also right there designing with me and I wouldn't do a thing without getting her opinion. I would be lost without the three of them and Thuy, who interprets our ideas and makes samples.

Do you have any words of wisdom for other people who find you an inspiration?

Hmmm, yes...find your own style, it's the only thing that comes easily. Then stick to it, no matter what.

It was lovely to be able to interview Candace, and visit her studio to see her lovely work in person. When this interview was being written, Candace was busy getting her clothing line together for review at the Internationally acclaimed ModaManhattan Juried Ready-To-Wear Clothing & Fashion Show.

If you've ever dreamed of designing and executing your own line of clothing using your sewing skills, this lady is a true inspiration!

- **Read Candace's interview about her lovely line of clothing in the Premier Issue of Faerie Magazine (www.faeriemagazine.com)**

- **Candace's clothing line will be on display at the ModaManhattan Juried Ready-to-Wear clothing show (www.modamanhattan.com)**

- **See the licensed line of clothing by Gypsy Moon, inspired by artist Amy Brown (www.gypsymoon.com)**

Bjarne og Leif Drews ~ Historical Costumes by Bjarne Drews
www.my-drewscostumes.dk

Bjarne is a creative man who lives in Denmark. He creates lovely embroidered works of art, as well as sumptuous historical costumes that would make one who never has an occasion to wear such a gown want one of his to wear just to feel like a Regency-era queen.

Bjarne studied costume design for four years, at an Arts and Crafts school in Copenhagen called, "Skolen For Brugskunst" linien for beklædningsformgivning (The school for Arts and Crafts the line for clothing). He graduated in 1980 after four years of study.

Bjarne hand dyes his own threads and ribbons, and pays close attention to details on all of his stunning work. He sells some creations by private commission. He is a highly respected artisan who posts frequently on the high-traffic Historical Costume e-list.

How long have you been sewing?
My mother used to sew a lot, and I always found it interesting to follow her work. When I was 8 years old, I started cross stitching; I made a bell pull with the wild birds of Denmark.

What inspired you to sew your works of art?
My parents bought a bigger house in a rural village and for the first time in my life I saw an old manor house which was outside the village. At first sight I got so interested in the place, and I rushed to the local library to find out more about this country house. I learned about its history, and got to see a lot of old portraits of people who used to live in this building. I grew very interested in the history of clothing because I found it very intriguing to study the clothes in the portraits.

When I got older I was involved in the restoration work started at the manor house when it was going to be opened to the public. I worked for free, because I wanted to help as much as I could, and I loved to be near this manor house.

In the meantime I got rather good at drawing and as I still had a lot of interest in the history of clothing, I enrolled in an arts and crafts school in Copenhagen. My study would lead me to be a costume designer. I studied for four years and I graduated in making costumes for some entertainers who performed Renaissance dances.

Those days my costumes didn't have much embroidery, as I didn't embroider a lot then. But I was making bobbin lace and used some of the laces on my costumes. Through the years of my costume making, I grew more and more fond of the costumes from the 18th century, and I have made this era my specialty these days. Also, I am involved with an historical reenactment society in Sweden, whose members reenact the time of Gustav III.

The embroidery simply is a necessity if you make costumes from this time. I now love embroidery so much now, that I actually have decided to stop my costuming and only make embroidered accessories for 18th century re-enactors.

When I look back of my life, I think I have fulfilled all of my dreams. I remember a special portrait of a lady courtesan. I wanted to recreate the court dress from the portrait.

I said to myself that I had to learn how to recreate such a dress. Well today I have, and my reconstructed dress is exhibited at the manor in front of the portrait where I was standing more than 35 years ago…

How do you advertise and market your skills?

The internet has been a great help to me. I have gained a lot of friends through costuming groups, and people have helped me to find the right materials I need when I embroider – sometimes it is difficult to find certain supplies here in Denmark. Many people from the lists I am a member of have gotten to know my work via my website. I have built my own website where people can see the things I make. This is the only way I advertise.

Do you have support or assistance from friends and family?

I don't have any support or assistance from family; I make everything myself, and I have a full time job besides my costume and embroidery business. So, every spare minute I have is used to make my art.

How do you cope with stress when you are really busy?

Most of the stress and frustration I get is when I am at my regular full time job, irritated that I have to do this, when I could sit back in my home and embroider or sew. Sometimes I get so many ideas when I am at work, and find it very annoying that I have to wait till I get home to try it out.

Embroidery is the best of relaxation you can get, it can heal all your stress and frustration away, and I really am hooked on it!

Bjarne's advice: Be in the business because you love the work, and success will follow.

Bjarne was gracious to give an interview for this book, and sets an example for other creative men who sew. Even though Bjarne is not out to make a fortune from his work, it goes to show that word of mouth advertising, and networking within a community of others who sew, is successful in marketing his lovely designs.

Part of Bjarne's impressive portfolio can be found at:
members.tripod.com/~DeeDee_Revia/bjarne1.html

View Bjarne's other website at:
home0.inet.tele.dk/drewscph

Ask Bjarne a question about his work by signing up for the Historical Costume e-list. In just about every post, something new about sewing, finding suppliers, and more, can be learned. Join this e-list at:
mail.indra.com/mailman/listinfo/h-costume

CQMagOnline profiled Bjarne for his lovely beadwork on a gown he had made for a client. This article can be found at:
www.cqmagonline.com/vol03iss03/articles/317

John French ~ DIY Slipcovers
www.diyslipcovers.com

John French runs a successful custom-tailored slipcover business and is the creator of instructional videos/DVDs for the beginner to learn the art of slipcovering. For two years, John taught slipcovering at MB Sewing Enterprises in Mesa, Arizona. Also, John has participated in slipcovering seminars at the Slipcover University with Pat Reese and at the Professional Drapery Workroom School in Ashville, N.C.

John French has been featured in the "Center Spotlight" at the Ethan Allen Showroom, Scottsdale, Arizona, and has done work for some of Dallas' top designers.

How long have you been involved in the sewing industry and what inspired you to start your business?
I have been in the sewing industry for 12 years. I began my business because I had seen other people make a good living from making custom tailored slipcovers. It worked for me because I am a creative person, a bit unconventional, I wanted my own business (to work for myself) and I truly believe that custom slipcovers are an excellent product/value.

I must have been a bit crazy because I decided to go into this before I new how to thread a needle. I have never looked back.

How did you start your business - did you start on a shoestring budget?
I started my business with almost no money and the most basic of sewing skills. I had just started some sewing classes when a lady commissioned me to make a set of cushions for a rattan sofa. Why not, I said. It just snow balled from that. So many people know nothing of sewing and are willing to pay someone to do it for them. Friends heard that

I had made a slipcover for myself and I started making covers for them at a reduced rate. I continued on this path for a year and then started my official business charging full rate. As I was learning, I purchased all my machines and equipment so I never was saddled with debt. I truly earned while I learned!

During the year, I made a trip to Seattle and took my portable machine with me because I was planning to make a cover for a family member. Well, neighbors found out about me and I started getting one job after another while I was away. I hated to come back! The business of slipcovers is very flexible!

Is there a great deal of sewing that goes into your products or is it mainly teaching?
My business is really two parts: custom tailored slipcovers and instructional videos/DVDs for the beginner.

Yes, there is a great deal of sewing that goes along with my custom slipcover business. Because I have so much business today, I have people who do much of the sewing for me. They usually sew at their own homes. The cutting of the covers is the unusual skill. It is not all that hard to find people to sew for me. It is all very basic sewing anyway.

My video business involves no sewing but it does take some of my time.

Do you have support/assistance from friends and family?

I get no assistance from my family. They simply put up with a lot of bolts of fabric and some occasional pieces of furniture placed through out the house!

If you could offer advice to a person - especially men - new to the sewing industry, what would it be?

The business of slipcovers is not hard although it might seem so. My first advice is to learn basic sewing skills or at least understand them if you do not plan to do your own sewing. Insist on delivering a quality product and charge well for your service. Maintain professionalism throughout every aspect of your business. Always remember that you have the option of saying "no thank you".

I would tell someone starting out in their own business today to **visualize** themselves as successful. Clearly see in your mind what your product looks like and what your customer looks like. Visualize getting paid and your customer complimenting your work. Visualize your phone ringing with a referral from a past customer. You are the only one who can hold you back!

How do you survive burn-out when you're really busy?

I love being busy. I thrive on it! Thank goodness I am busy! I insist on staying fit and go to the gym regularly. I don't work once I get tired especially at night. I am much better in the morning! I don't take on more "non profitable work". If I find something non profitable, I learn from my mistake and avoid letting it happen again. I try not to beat myself up; who needs that!

Visit John's impressive website to see some of his work at:

www.diyslipcovers.com

John has posted several informative articles to his website that are about creating slipcovers. There is also a comprehensive tips and hints section, along with a "questions answered" area.

Take a video course and learn many different levels of slipcover design and construction.

Conclusion

Embarking on a new business endeavor may be one of the most exciting things you will ever do. To be in control of your own destiny, and to be the initiator of your own success, and freedom are some of the positive aspects of owning your own business.

Whether you decide to start your business on your own—or if you have a business partner to help you with decisions—staying organized, being clear about your business and marketing strategies, and sticking with your plan, will help make you successful.

Get involved with your local small business support venues, such as the Small Business Administration, networking groups, and your local chamber of commerce. Consistent marketing and networking will prove to be a rewarding method of promoting your business. Communicating regularly with these groups and forming contacts with as many people in the sewing industry as possible will help you to find creative ways to give your company and its products continuous exposure and a better chance for success.

Along the way – remind yourself often of what mythologist Joseph Campbell once said, "Follow your bliss and doors will open where there were no doors before."

Inspirations &
Affirmations

"Effective people are not problem-minded; they're opportunity-minded. They feed opportunities and starve problems." —Stephen Covey

"If you accommodate others, you will be accommodating yourself."
—Chinese proverb

"There are few, if any, jobs in which ability alone is sufficient. Needed, also, are loyalty, sincerity, enthusiasm and team play." —William B. Given, Jr.

"The big secret in life is that there is no big secret. Whatever your goal, you can get there if you're willing to work." —Oprah Winfrey

"Giving people a little more than they expect is a good way to get back more than you'd expect." —Robert Half

"And the trouble is, if you don't risk anything, you risk even more." —Erica Jong

"If you mean to profit, learn to please." —Winston Churchill

"Don't agonize. Organize." —Florynce Kennedy

"Keep away from people who try to belittle your ambitions. Small people always do that, but the really great make you feel that you, too, can become great."
—Mark Twain

"People become really quite remarkable when they start thinking that they can do things. When they believe in themselves they have the first secret of success."
—Norman Vincent Peale

"Sometimes the only thing we do to avoid success is refuse to be energetic on our own behalf." —Barbara Sher

"It never occurs to me that there are things that I can't do." —Whoopi Goldberg

"If you want your life to be more rewarding, you have to change the way you think." —Oprah Winfrey

APPENDIX A

Suppliers & Resources

We do not endorse these businesses in any way, nor are these paid endorsements. It is up to you to research and hopefully benefit from these resources. This information is current as of the publishing date of this book.

Coding: It is difficult to define websites with just a few codes. Some websites offer more than what is listed. B = Garment Bags; E = Education, books, classes; EQ = Equipment & Furniture; ES = Embroidery Supply; F = Fabric & More; FS = Full line of supplies; L = Garment Labels; N = Notions, P = Patterns, Design Software; Q = Quilting Supply; S = Specialty; Tools, & More; U = Upholstery Supply

Vendors of Fabrics, Notions, Garment Labels & More

Vendor Name	URL/Web Address	Sales Code
5 T's Embroidery Supply	www.5ts.com	ES
Able Labels of America	www.ablelabels.com	L
Academy of Fashion Designs	www.aofdesign.com	E
Academy of Fine Sewing & Design	www.finesewing.com	E
Acme Country Fabrics	www.acmecountryfabrics.com	F, N
Acme Notions	www.acmenotions.com	N
Alpha Impressions	www.alphaimpressions.com	L
American Sewing Center	www.american-sewing.com	EQ
American Trim & Upholstery Supply	www.atrim.com	N, U
Apple Annie Fabrics	www.appleanniefabrics.com	F
Arrowmont School	www.arrowmont.org	E
Aurora Silk	www.aurorasilk.com	F
Baer Fabrics	www.baerfabrics.com	F
Banasch's	www.banaschs.com	B, EQ, F, N
Barb Originals	www.barboriginals.com	P, F, E
Barudan America, Inc.	www.barudan.com	EQ
BBlack & Sons	www.bblackandsons.com	F, N
Beacon Fabric & Notions	www.beaconfabric.com	F, N
Bead Different Embroidery	www.beaddifferentembroidery.com	ES
Bernina	www.berninausa.com	EQ
Bramaker Supply	www.bramakers.com	N, F
Bullard Designs	www.bullarddesigns.com	ES,N
Burda (Germany)	www.burdamode.com	P
Burda World of Fashion	www.glpnews.com/crafts.html	P
Buttons & Bolts & Fabrics	www.buttonsnboltsfabrics.com	F, N
Buttons NW	www.buttonsofnw.com	N
Calontir Trim	www.calontirtrim.com	N
Candlelight Valley Fabrics	www.candlelightvalleyfabrics.com	F
Christine Jonson Patterns	www.cjpatterns.com	P
Clothing Labels 4u.com	www.clothinglabels4u.com	L
Clotilde	www.clotilde.com	FS
Cotton Plus	www.organiccottonplus.com	F
Create for Less	www.createforless.com	FS

B = Garment Bags; E = Education, books, classes; EQ = Equipment & Furniture; ES = Embroidery Supply; F = Fabric & More; FS = Full line of supplies; L = Garment Labels; N = Notions, P = Patterns, Design Software; Q = Quilting Supply; S = Specialty; Tools, & More; U = Upholstery Supply

Vendor Name	URL/Web Address	Sales Code
Creekside Embroidery Designs	www.creeksidedesigns.com	ES
Curran Designers Fabrics	www.currandesignersfabrics.com	F
Cutting Corners, Inc.	www.cuttinglinedesigns.com	F, P
Darr, Incorporated	www.darrsewnotions.com	N
Dawn Anderson Designs	www.dawnandersondesigns.com	P, F
Delectable Mountain Cloth	www.delectablemountain.com	F
Delta Sewing Furniture	www.deltasewing.com	EQ
Denver Fabrics	www.denverfabrics.com	F
Design to Fit Patterns, Inc.	www.designtofit.com	P
Dharma Trading Co	www.dharmatrading.com	N
Discount Fabrics USA	www.discountfabricsusa.com	F
Distinctive Fabric	www.distinctivefabric.com	F
Distinctive Sewing Supplies	www.distinctivesewing.com	FS
Doll Artist's Workshop	www.minidolls.com	F, N
DMC Thread	www.dmc-usa.com	N
Do It Yourself Slipcovers	www.diyslipcovers.com	E
Earth Guild	www.earthguild.com	N
Embroider This!	www.embroiderthis.com	ES
Embroidery Arts	www.embroideryarts.com	ES
Embroidery Library	www.emblibrary.com	ES
eQuilter.com	www.equilter.com	Q
Estees Fabrics	www.estees-fabrics.com	F
Eva Dress	www.evadress.com	P, N, F
Fabric Dot Com	www.fabricdotcom.com	F
Fabric Gallery	www.fabricgallery.net	F, N, P
Fabric.com	www.fabric.com	F
FabricDirect.com	www.fabricdirect.com	F
Fabrics-Store	www.fabrics-store.com	F
Fabulous Fit Dress Forms	www.fabulousfit.com	EQ
Fare Tahiti Fabrics	www.faretahiti.com	F
Farthingale's	www.farthingales.on.ca	N
Fire Mountain Gems	www.firemountaingems.com	N
Fletcher Farm School	www.fletcherfarm.org	E
Folkwear	www.folkwear.com	P
French Connections	www.french-nc.com	F, N
Fuhng Satin Co., Inc.	www.fuhngsatin.com	F
Gaffney Fabrics, Inc.	www.gaffneyfabrics.com	F
Gayfeather Fabrics	www.gayfeatherfabrics.com	F
General Label Mfg.	www.generallabel.com	L
Ginny's Fine Fabrics	www.ginnysfinefabrics.com	F
Grannd Garb	www.grannd.com	N
Great Copy Patterns	www.greatcopy.com	P
Greenberg-Hammer	www.greenberg-hammer.com	N
Haberman Fabrics	www.habermanfabrics.com	F
Hancock Fabrics	www.hancockfabrics.com	FS
Hands of the Hills	www.handsofthehills.com	F, N
Hobby Ware	www.hobbyware.com	P
Home Sew	www.homesew.com	N
Homespun Wide Fabrics	www.homespunfabrics.com	F
Husqvarna/Viking	www.husqvarnaviking.com	EQ
Islander Sewing Systems	www.islandersewing.com	E, P
Jacquard Products	www.jacquardproducts.com	N
J-Caroline Creative	www.jcarolinecreative.com	N

B = Garment Bags; E = Education, books, classes; EQ = Equipment & Furniture; ES = Embroidery Supply; F = Fabric & More;
FS = Full line of supplies; L = Garment Labels; N = Notions, P = Patterns, Design Software; Q = Quilting Supply; S = Specialty;
Tools, & More; U = Upholstery Supply

Vendor Name	URL/Web Address	Sales Code
Jo-Ann Fabrics	www.joann.com	FS
Josephine's Dry Goods	www.josephinesdrygoods.com	F
Joyce Upholstery	www.joyceupholstery.com	F
K Trimming	www.ktrimming.com	N
Kandi Corp	www.l-orna.com	N, Q
Kay Woods	www.ebaystores.com/renaissancefabrics	F
Ken's Sewing Center	www.kenssewingcenter.com	EQ
La Fred	www.lafred.com	P
LesBon Ribbon	www.lesbonribbon.com	N
Loes Hinse Design	www.loeshinsedesign.com	P
Lorraine Torrence Designs	www.lorrainetorrence.com	F, Q
Lumenlight.com	www.lumenlight.com	EQ
Make Me! Fabrics	www.makemefabrics.com	F, N
Malden Mills	www.maldenmillsstore.com	F
Manhattan Fabrics	www.manhattanfabrics.com	F
Manhattan Wardrobe Supply	www.wardrobesupplies.com	N
Michael's Fabrics	www.michaelsfabrics.com	F
Mill End Store	www.millendstore.com	F
MJ Trim	www.mjtrim.com	N
Monterey Mills	www.montereymills.com	F
My Twin Dress Forms	www.mytwindressforms.com	EQ
MyNotions.com	www.mynotions.com	N
Name Maker, Inc.	www.namemaker.com	L
Nancy's Notions	www.nancysnotions.com	FS
Neue Mode (Germany)	www.sullivans.net	P, F, N
Newark Dressmaker Supply	www.newarkdress.com	FS
Oriental Silk Company	www.orientalsilk.com	F
Ott-Lite Technology	www.ott-lite.com	EQ
Ottobre Design	www.ottobredesign.com	P
Rain City Publishing	www.raincitypublishing.com	E
Ribbon Girls	www.ribbongirls.net	N
Rit Dye	www.ritdye.com	N, E
Royalwood, Ltd.	www.royalwoodltd.com	N
Sadia's Designs	www.sadiasews.com	Q, ES
Sailrite Kits	www.sailrite.com	E, N
Sawyer Brook Fabrics	www.sawyerbrook.com	F
Seattle Fabrics	www.seattlefabrics.com	F
Sew Thankful	www.sewthankful.com	N
Sew-Brite	www.sew-brite.com	EQ
SewinginUSA.com	www.sewinginusa.com	EQ
Silk Connection	www.silkconnection.com	F
Silver Reed Knitting Machine	www.silverreed.com	EQ
Simplicity	www.simplicity.com	P, E
Sparkling Impressions	www.sparkling-impressions.com	N, P
St. Theresa Textile Trove	www.sttheresatextile.com	F, Q
Steinlauf & Stoller	www.steinlaufandstoller.com	N, L, EQ
Sterling Name Tape (Labels)	www.sterlingnametape.com	L
Stitchitize Embroidery	www.stitchitize.com	ES
Stretch & Sew Fabrics	www.stretchandsewmn.com	F, E
Stretch House, Inc.	www.stretchhouse.com	F
String Codes Design	pattern.stringcodes.com	P
Sue's Sparklers	www.suessparklers.com	N
SyFabrics	www.syfabrics.com	F

B = Garment Bags; E = Education, books, classes; EQ = Equipment & Furniture; ES = Embroidery Supply; F = Fabric & More; FS = Full line of supplies; L = Garment Labels; N = Notions, P = Patterns, Design Software; Q = Quilting Supply; S = Specialty; Tools, & More; U = Upholstery Supply

Vendor Name	URL/Web Address	Sales Code
Textile Studio Patterns	www.textilestudiofabrics.com	P, F
Thai Silks!	www.thaisilks.com	F
The Button Drawer	www.buttondrawer.com	N
The Cotton Boll	www.thecottonboll.com	E
The Couture Sewing School	www.susankhalje.com	E
The Electric Quilt Company	www.electricquilt.com	Q
The Green Pepper	www.thegreenpepper.com	P, F, N
The Jane A. Sassaman Co.	www.janesassaman.com	Q, E
The Quilted Dragon	www.quilted-dragon.com	Q
The Rainshed	www.therainshed.com	F, P, N
The Sewing Place	www.thesewingplace.com	F, P, N
The Sewing Workshop	www.sewingworkshop.com	P, N
Sulky Thread	www.sulky.com	N, E
The Wooly Thread	www.woolythread.com	N
ThreadArt	www.threadart.com	ES, Q, N
Timmel Fabrics	www.timmelfabrics.com	F
Tinsel Trading Co	www.tinseltrading.com	N
TrimFabric.com	www.fabrictv.com	F, N
Ultra Style Designs	www.ultrastyledesigns.com	F, N
Uline	www.uline.com	B
Universal Presser Foot Lifter	www.presserfootlifter.com	EQ
Utica Thread	www.uticathread.com	N
Vestis Books	www.vestisbooks.com	E
Waechters	www.waechters.com	F, N, P
Wild Ginger Software, Inc.	www.wildginger.com	P
WMN Ginsburg	www.ginstrim.com	N
You Can Make It, Inc.	www.youcanmakeit.com	E
ZipperSource	www.zippersource.com	N
Zundt Design	www.zundtdesign.com	ES

Sewing Resources & Informational Websites

SewingCity	www.sewingcity.com
Lily Abello's Sewing Resource Guide	www.lilyabello.com
The Home Sewing Association	www.sewing.org
Quilter's News Network	www.quiltersnewsnetwork.com
Threads Magazine	www.threadsmagazine.com
Quiltropolis e-Lists	www.quiltropolis.com
Sew What's New	sew-whats-new.com
Pattern Review	sewing.patternreview.com
Sewing at About.com	sewing.about.com
American Sewing Guild	www.asg.org
Home Sewing Association	www.sewing.org
Sewing.com	www.sewing.com
See It, Sew It	www.seeitsewit.com
Sewing Web	www.sewingweb.com
Sewing World Commons	www.sewingworld.com
Sew Much More Info	www.sewmuchmoreinfo.com
Fabrics.net	www.fabrics.net
SewOrganized	www.seworganized.com
Historic Costume e-List	mail.indra.com/mailman/listinfo/h-costume

Small Business Resources

Small Business Administration	www.sba.gov
Entrepreneur Magazine	www.entrepreneur.com
PayPal	www.paypal.com
Western Union	www.westernunion.com
Card Service International	www.cardservicesales.com
Business Owners Idea Café	www.businessownersideacafe.com
Home Business Magazine	www.homebusinessmag.com
Amazon.com	www.amazon.com
Barnes & Noble Online	www.barnesandnoble.com
Inc.om	www.inc.com
Business Plan Pro (Palo Alto Software)	www.paloalto.com
Office Depot	www.officedepot.com
Staples	www.staples.com
Stamps.com	www.stamps.com

Web Design Resources

Scrub The Web	www.scrubtheweb.com
Steve's Templates	www.steves-templates.com
BraveNet	www.bravenet.com
Dotster	www.dotster.com
Hypermart Web Hosting	www.hypermart.com
Pair Web Hosting	www.pair.com
Web Alley	www.weballey.net
Google	www.google.com
AltaVista	www.altavista.com
Yahoo!	www.yahoo.com
MSN (Microsoft)	www.msn.com
Lycos	www.lycos.com
Webcrawler	www.webcrawler.com
AOL (America Online)	www.aol.com

Auction sites
----

eBay	www.ebay.com
Overstock.com	www.overstock.com
Amazon.com	www.amazon.com
Yahoo Auctions	www.yahoo.com

Shipping Resources

United States Post Office	www.usps.com
Federal Express	www.fedex.com
United Parcel Service	www.ups.com
PaperMart	www.papermart.com
U-Haul	www.uhaul.com

Project Name:

Materials	Quantity Needed	Unit Price + Shipping	Total Price	Vendor	Notes
Labor					
Total cost					
Customer Price					
Profit					

APPENDIX C

This sample template is an illustration of an organized table structure for a webpage. Using tables will insure that your data is kept in consistent order throughout your website. The lines are used here for illustrative purposes only, and you can always use colors, imagery, or other methods to design your website's look and feel. The structure is built by using one large table, centered, width set to 750 pixels. Another table, set to 100% width is placed inside of the first table. It has four rows, and three columns. Cell padding is set to 5 for all tables. The top and bottom two rows are merged cells, so that a banner image will fit, as well as lines of text to span across the bottom of the page, which are centered. Navigation buttons may be placed anywhere, including across the top, down either side, or the bottom of the page, using another row.

Your business logo/banner here		
Navigation buttons or links here	You could place a row of navigational tabs here instead of down the left side Webpage Body Text	Affiliate ads, special promotions, pictures, links, informational text, etc.
Home | Products | Services | Shipping | Sizing | About Us | Legal | Sitemap | Contact		
Copyright information. All rights reserved.		

Do not forget to edit your page properties. Page properties determine the page title, which viewers see when they enter and browse your website, as well as metatags and keywords—all of which are essential for proper search engine ranking.

APPENDIX D

I. Cover sheet
II. Statement of purpose
III. Table of contents
   - The Business
     1. Description of business
     2. Marketing
     3. Competition analysis
     4. Operating procedures
     5. Personnel
     6. Business insurance
   - Financial Data
     1. Loan applications
     2. Capital equipment and inventory & supply list
     3. Balance sheet
     4. Breakeven analysis
     5. Pro-forma income projections (profit & loss statements)
     6. Three-year summary
     7. Detail by month, first year
     8. Detail by quarters, second and third years
     9. Assumptions upon which projections were based
     10. Pro-forma cash flow
IV. Supporting Documents
     1. Tax returns of principals for last three years
     2. Personal financial statement (all banks have these forms)
     3. Copy of proposed lease or purchase agreement for building space
     4. Copy of licenses and other legal documents
     5. Copy of résumés of all principals
     6. Copies of letters of intent from suppliers, etc.

This sample page is not to be considered as legal advice in any form. You may use this sample page as a reference for developing your own legal policies for your business, and adjust it as you wish to suit your needs for your website. Have your attorney or legal counsel review your final draft to insure that it follows your state's legal guidelines.

Welcome to [YourStoreName.com].

[YourStoreName.com] and its affiliates provide their services to you subject to the following notices, terms, and conditions. In addition, when you use any [YourStoreName.com] services you will be subject to the rules, guidelines, policies, terms, and conditions applicable to such service.

Copyright

All content included on this site, such as text, graphics, logos, button icons, images, audio clips, software, and the compilation (meaning the collection, arrangement, and assembly) of all content on this site, is the property of [YourStoreName.com] or its content suppliers and protected by U.S. and international copyright laws. All software used on this site is the property of [YourStoreName.com] or its software suppliers and protected by U.S. and international copyright laws. The content and software on this site may be used as a shopping, selling, and e-card resource. Any other use, including the reproduction, modification, distribution, transmission, republication, display, or performance, of the content on this site is strictly prohibited.

Trademarks

[YourStoreName.com] and [Your Store Name] are registered trademarks of [Your Store Name], in the United States and other countries. [YourStoreName.com] graphics, logos, and service names are trademarks of [Your Store Name]. [Your Store Name]'s trademarks may not be used in connection with any product or service that is not [YourStoreName.com]'s in any manner that is likely to cause confusion among customers, or in any manner that disparages or discredits [YourStoreName.com].

Use of Website

This site or any portion of this site may not be reproduced, duplicated, copied, sold, resold, or otherwise exploited for any commercial purpose that is not expressly permitted by [YourStoreName.com]. [YourStoreName.com] and its affiliates reserve the right to refuse service, terminate accounts, and/or cancel orders in its discretion, including, without limitation, if [YourStoreName.com] believes that customer conduct violates applicable law or is harmful to the interests of [YourStoreName.com] and its affiliates.

Privacy

Registration data and other information about you and your usage of [YourStoreName.com] are subject to our privacy policy. Email addresses provided by you may be used by us to send you information on an intermittent basis. You may opt out of any further email by simply replying and requesting to be removed from our mailing list. Our mailing list will not be shared with any party outside the [YourStoreName.com] organization for any reason. Our monthly newsletter is an opt-in feature, so you will not receive it unless you specifically request it. [YourStoreName.com] will not knowingly solicit data from children, and will never knowingly market to children. [YourStoreName.com] does not store or share confidential data such as credit cards, expiration dates, or any other financial data about our customers.

Reviews, Public Forums, & Comments

[YourStoreName.com] enables visitors to its site to post reviews of and comments on products featured on the site. If you post reviews or comments on the site, you grant [YourStoreName.com] and its affiliates a non-exclusive, royalty-free, perpetual, irrevocable, and fully sub-licensable right to use, reproduce, modify, adapt, publish, translate, create derivative works from, distribute, and display such reviews and comments throughout the world in any media. You also grant [YourStoreName.com] and its affiliates and sub-licensees the right to use the name that you submit with any review or comment, if any, in connection with such review or comment.

Returns

We gladly accept unused merchandise that bears no sign of wear or damage and that has all original tags attached.

Customers must obtain a return authorization number (RA) before merchandise may be returned. Customers may e-mail or call us to obtain an RA number.

The RA number must be clearly written on the outside of the package, or the package will be not be accepted. We are not responsible for damages that occur after delivery. Shipping costs are paid for by the customer.

There are no returns for any item which is customized for size. If you should decide to return an item, we ask that it be sent back insured for the full value (the amount you paid for the item) via a traceable method (UPS, Federal Express, etc.)

Once we have received the returned garment, we will provide an exchange or issue a store credit. Shipping and handling charges are non-refundable for returned or exchanged items.

Merchandise may be returned for exchange or credit refund within ten business days of the receipt of purchase. Returns will not be accepted after this time. Unauthorized returns will not be accepted under any circumstances, and unmarked parcels (without an RA number) will be returned to the sender.

Risk of Loss

All items purchased from [YourStoreName.com] are made pursuant to a shipment contract. This means that the risk of loss and title for such items pass to you upon our delivery to the carrier.

Advertisers

Your correspondence or business dealings with, or participation in promotions of, advertisers found on or by way of [YourStoreName.com] including payment and delivery of related goods or services, and any other terms, conditions, warranties, or representations associated with such dealings, are solely between you and such advertiser. [YourStoreName.com] shall not be held responsible in any manner for transactions between members of the site and advertisers. Notifying [YourStoreName.com] of misrepresented advertisers and sponsors is at the discretion of [YourStoreName.com] members. Complaints regarding advertisers may be directed to webmaster@ [YourStoreName.com] for immediate review.

Disclaimer

This site is provided by [YourStoreName.com] on an "as is" basis. [YourStoreName.com] makes no representations or warranties of any kind, express or implied, as to the operation of the site or the information, content, materials, or products included on this site. To the full extent permissible by applicable law, [YourStoreName.com] disclaims all warranties, express or implied, including, but not limited to, implied warranties of merchantability and fitness for a particular purpose. [YourStoreName.com] will not be liable for any damages or any kind arising from the use of this site, including, but not limited to direct, indirect, incidental, punitive, and consequential damages.

Applicable Law

This site is created and controlled by [YourStoreName.com] in the State of [Your State], USA. As such, the laws of the State of [Your State] will govern these disclaimers, terms, and conditions, without giving effect to any principles of conflicts of laws. We reserve the right to make changes to our site and these disclaimers, terms, and conditions at any time.

Our Contact Information

[YourStoreName.com]
[Your Phone Number]
[Your Fax Number]
[Your Store Name]
[Your Address]
[Your City, State, Zip]
webmaster@[YourStoreName.com]

9873845R0

Made in the USA
Lexington, KY
05 June 2011